The Jewish Self-Image in the West

The Jewish Self-Image
in the West

Michael Berkowitz

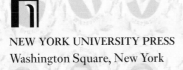

NEW YORK UNIVERSITY PRESS
Washington Square, New York

For Debby, Rachel and Stephen, with love

First published in the U. S. A. in 2000 by
NEW YORK UNIVERSITY PRESS
Washington Square, New York, NY 10003

Copyright © Michael Berkowitz 2000

Series design by Humphrey Stone

Printed and bound in Great Britain by Biddles Ltd,
Guildford and King's Lynn

Library of Congress Cataloging-in-Publication Data
Berkowitz, Michael.
The Jewish self-image in the west / Michael Berkowitz
p.cm.
Includes bibliographical references and index.
ISBN 0-8147-9861-6 (cloth)
1. Jews – Portraits. 2. Jews – Biography. 3. Jews – Identity. 4. Zionists – Portraits.
5. Jews – Europe, Western – Social conditions – 19th century. 6. Jews – Europe,
Western – Social conditions – 20th century. 7. Jews – United States – Social
conditions – 19th century. 8. Jews – United States – Social conditions – 20th century.
9. Jews – Politics and government – 19th century. 10. Jews – Politics and government – 20th
century. 11. Self-perception – Religious aspects – Judaism. I. Title.
DS115 B38 2000
920'.009292401821--dc21   99-041831

Contents

Yes, the cosmopolitan spirit sprang from the soil of Judaea, and Christ, who was really a Jew, founded a propaganda organization for international brotherhood.

HEINRICH HEINE, on Shakespeare's 'Merchant of Venice'

O do not lose heart, beautiful Messiah, who wishes to redeem not only Israel, as the superstitious Jews imagine, but the whole of suffering mankind!

HEINRICH HEINE, 'Rabbi Menasse ben Naphtali of Crakow'

The scoff, the curse – his people's heritage –
Have left upon his shrunken face their sting;
His eyes gleam like those of some hunted thing,
Against whose life implacable war men wage.
We read the Jew's face as one reads a page
Of his own nation's history, for there cling
About its lines, deep-worn with suffering,
The traces still of Israel's lordly age.

Attributed to FFM, epigraph of Karl Emil Franzos, *The Jews of Barnow: Stories*

Whatever I have to say of Herzl, the unforgettable, I have tried to put into the several portraits which I have made of the physical man. I know that my attempts have fallen short, for our leader was a man of superhuman beauty. And I confess freely that it was this divine gift of beauty which left the deepest and most enduring impress on my mind.

HERMANN STRUCK, 'As an Artist Saw Him: The Man of Sorrows and the Seer', in *Theodor Herzl: A Memorial*, ed. Meyer W. Weisgal

I was not a redhead for nothing. That summer [after the First World War] I attended the annual meeting of the [New York] State Federation of Labour as a delegate, as I had done ever since [it] existed. I asked for the floor during one of the sessions and told the delegates what [James P. Holland, president of the organization] had done. I accused him of bearing false witness against me. I said that I did not think the president of a trade-union organization would try to blacken the character of any of its members and that I had always believed that we must stick together. I received a terrific hand when I sat down.

ROSE SCHNEIDERMAN with LUCY GOLDTHWAITE, *All for One*

An assimilated Jew and a hunchback were passing a synagogue. 'I used to be a Jew once', says the Jew. 'Yes', the hunchback says, ' – and I used to be a hunchback.'

Attributed to GROUCHO MARX

Frontispiece Detail of illus. 70.

Acknowledgements

This book originated in a discussion with Sander Gilman, over a bowl of borscht, in a restaurant that no longer exists in central Ohio. I wish to thank him for helping me nurture this study. Along the way to its completion several individuals and institutions lent crucial support. A grant from the Littauer Foundation facilitated the bulk of research. I would like to thank, as well, the Committee on Jewish Studies at the University of Chicago, under whose auspices I was a visitor. In Hyde Park I greatly benefited from my association with Michael Fishbane, Eric Santner, Ralph Austen, Philip Bohlman, Peter Novick, Michael Geyer, Miriam Hansen, John Boyer, Matti Bunzl, Billy Vaughn, Andrew Patner, John Woods, Sharon Wood, Christopher Simmons, Shirli Brautbar, Daniel Greene, Gabriel Finder, Cherilyn Lacy, Eden Rosenbush, and David Dennis. At University College London my departmental colleagues John Klier, Ada Rapoport-Albert, Mark Geller, Tsila Ratner, Hugh Denman, Tali Loewenthal, John Fox, Neil Lochery, Sally Gold, Joanna Newman, Sarah Sviri, and Leon Yudkin provide a most congenial and stimulating environment. In the midst of writing I enjoyed – which truly is the right word, in this case – a visiting scholarship at St John's College, Oxford. Among those colleagues, world-wide, who deserve mention for their encouragement and assistance are Leslie Adelson, Seth Wolitz, Daniel Boyarin, David Sorkin, Daniel Soyer, Laurence Silberstein, John Hoberman, Andrew Bachman, David Brenner, Laurence Baron, Paul L. Rose, David Luft, Claudio Fogu, Ezra Mendelsohn, Michael Brenner, Marc Weiner, Raphael Loewe, David Solomon, Joel Gereboff, Charles Dellheim, Dagmar Lorenz, Nicholas Howe, Alon Confino, Alan Steinweis, Jacob Meskin, Thomas Bird, Charles Atkinson, Fred Siegel, Richard Freund, Noah Isenberg, Dorothee Schneider, Harry Liebersohn, David N. Myers, Joel Berkowitz, Keith Pickus, David Rechter, Howard M. Sachar, Steven Kale, Marshall Stevenson, Stuart Lishan, Lewis Bateman, Christopher Browning, Ross McKibbin, Simon Whittaker, Desmond King, Lawrence Goldman, Angela Williams,

David Gibbins, Fareda Banda, Ian Simmons, George Richardson, Eli Shibi-Shai, Shalom Goldman, David Miller, Neil Jacobs, Sean Martin, Larry Bell, Mary McCune, Michael Bryant, Aaron Retisch, Lisa Jenschke, Ernest Schlesinger, John Efron, Ruth Rischin, Moses Rischin, Chimen Abramsky, Ammiel Alcalay, Derek Penslar, Zev Weiss, Mark Astaire, Ben Fortna, Barry Davies, Tamar Fox, James Renton, Matthew Martinson, Samantha Kowalski, Jonathan Lelliott, Lia Kahn-Zajtmann, Juliet Summerfield, Sarah Jennings, Ian Lilicrapp, Friedhelm v. Notz, Sam Norich, Barry Pateman, Paulette Manos, Oliver Leaman, Michael Leaman, Andrea Belloli, Harry Gilonis, Karen Anderson Howes and Gerard J. P. O'Daley. I also would like to acknowledge those who are no longer present to receive such thanks: colleagues Marilyn Waldman and Michael Weitzman, my teacher Sterling Fishman, and my mentor, George L. Mosse.

I continue to reap treasures from my original and ongoing research home, the Central Zionist Archives in Jerusalem, and wish to thank Pinchas Selinger, Reuven Koffler, and Yoram Mayorek again. At the American Jewish Archives in Cincinnati Kevin Profitt was extremely helpful, as were Fruma Mohrer at YIVO, Brad Sabin Hill at Oxford, Joseph Galron in Columbus, Carol Siegel at the Jewish Museum in Finchley, and Dalia Tracz, at the Jewish Studies Library of University College London. I am fortunate to have had access to learned professionals and interesting collections in Tel Aviv, Jerusalem, Los Angeles, Columbus, Cincinnati, Amsterdam, New York, Oxford, and London.

To my family I can only begin to express my love and thanks.

1 Introduction

This book investigates modern Jewish iconography, especially pertaining to the Jewish experience with political movements in the United States, Britain and Western Europe from 1881 to 1939. In contrast to most works relating Jews and images its emphasis is not on anti-Semitism.[1] I have attempted to look over the shoulder of previous generations of Western Jews, to appreciate how they perceived representations of themselves. Properly speaking this is not a sounding in 'Jewish art' or 'Jewish photography',[2] but rather an interpretation of applications of art, graphics and photography, over time, which accompanied and fostered the ethnic mobilization of Western Jews in the realm of popular culture. To be sure, the teachings of the Frankfurt School and the resurgence of interest in Walter Benjamin have underscored the anti-humanist and anti-Semitic consequences of mass culture, for commercial and explicitly political purposes.[3] Yet in the decades before the Holocaust, organized segments of Jewry enthusiastically appropriated modern media in order to exert a greater control over their lives as well as to realize their humanity more fully. It is hoped that this study of how Jews visualized themselves is suggestive for exploring how religious identities become secularized, and for questioning the permeable membrane between the secular and religious, as well as between everyday life and ideology. It also engages the complex relationship of images, and the mediation of images, to identity formation and ethnic politics. After all, it is past time that scholars of social sciences and humanities should seek to apprehend the ways Jews saw themselves and the ongoing significance of their self-recreation.[4]

There exists a large body of scholarly literature showing how iconography, mainly in the form of the Aryan stereotype, was wielded against the Jews, which eventually helped facilitate the destruction of European Jewry in the Holocaust. Jews were portrayed as embodying and spreading 'degeneracy' which, anti-Semites warned, threatened fatally to contaminate the non-Jewish majorities of Germany and other nations.[5] Yet one need not focus on the most renowned arenas of

Jew-hatred – Nazi Germany, fin-de-siècle Vienna, or anti-Dreyfusard France – to demonstrate that there was a widely shared, visually oriented discourse that gave credence to and exaggerated anti-Semitic allegations. This is not to suggest that all varieties of anti-Semitism were uniform in content or intensity, but that there were, across the West, common elements in the ways Jews were negatively perceived by non-Jewish societies. In Britain and the United States, notably, this was tempered by the degree to which Jews in major cities were valued for their 'voting strength', however much they tended to become 'a political football'.[6]

Even the photojournalistic 'social reformers' of early twentieth-century Britain and the United States reinforced derogatory stereotypes of Jews that, at least in part, ascribed the wretchedness of their material circumstances to hereditary proclivities, intra-Jewish exploitation and collective stubbornness. The Jews' maintenance of their historical-religious identity was derided as essential to their deplorable state. 'The Jewish quarter of New York', wrote Hutchins Hapgood in 1902, is thought 'to be a place of poverty, dirt, ignorance and immorality – the seat of the sweat-shop, the tenement house, and where "red-lights" sparkle at night, where people are queer and repulsive'.[7] Wherever Jews were found to live in densely packed blocks, and the ranks of those moving out were replenished by immigrants from Eastern Europe, it is not difficult to find roughly interchangeable descriptions. Adolf Hitler's haunting line about the caftan-Jew in Vienna would not have been out of place in similar memoirs of urban centres from Central Europe to the Midwestern United States.

Although Jews themselves routinely employed the term 'ghetto' to depict their pre-eminent domains in New York and elsewhere, they did not tend to call the Lower East Side 'Jewtown' as did the influential Jacob Riis. Riis believed that Jewish 'cunning' ultimately would enable their appropriation of the 'houses and lands of their persecutors'.[8] Riis wrote that when one enters 'Jewtown' there is 'No need of saying where we are. The jargon of the streets, the signs of the sidewalk, the manner and dress of the people, their unmistakable physiognomy, betray their race at every step. Men with queer skull-caps, venerable beard and the outlandish long-skirted caftan of the Russian Jew, elbow the ugliest and the handsomest women in the land.'[9] Interestingly, Riis was known for befriending the famed Jewish social worker and reformer, Lillian Wald (illus. 1).[10] Superficially, Wald's beaming countenance and her compassion for Jewish immigrants could scarcely have been more alien to Riis's jaundiced view and scathing indictment. But Wald, too, prized the goal of Jewish conformity to the prevalent

1 Lillian Wald (1886–1938): Born in Cincinnati, Ohio to a well-off German-Jewish family, Wald dedicated herself to the Jews of the Lower East Side of New York City. Despite her ambivalence about Jewishness, she was among the most compassionate chroniclers of ghetto life.

middle-class Gentile expectations. Their common ground, most likely, was Riis's support for moral and hygienic clean-up efforts as championed by Wald.[11]

In Britain the reformers' analyses were much the same as that of Riis. John Tagg writes that, in the city of Leeds, the Jewish community quickly gained leverage in municipal politics around the turn of the century. Nevertheless they 'remained a target of prolonged racialist agitation', based on fears that Jews undercut wages and that they received public favours in the allocation of housing and workplaces. 'On several occasions' these charges led to 'gang fights and rioting'. What is retrospectively perceived as dispassionate 'documentary' photography, Tagg shows, allied photography with anti-Semitism in the name of 'slum clearance'.[12] Of course, Jews were not the only immigrant group stigmatized in this way; Italians, among others, were said to exploit their own people, and even their children, for the sake of naked 'greed'.[13] What is remarkable about non-Jewish observations about Jews, however, is their consistency in disparate national settings.

As is well known, the most virulent manifestations of anti-Semitism aimed to limit severely the Jews' exercise of economic, political and intellectual liberty. The messages directed at them implied that Jews ought voluntarily to wean themselves from Jewish ways and relinquish the bad habits that had been exacerbated by living among themselves. Local and state authorities were implored to take vigorous action to transform them along the lines of the non-Jewish majority. There was no value attributed to the Jews' sustaining themselves as a distinctive, corporate entity, except to sponsor a charitable infrastructure to raise the status of their most destitute urchins – and therefore to help clean up the streets.[14]

Among the Jews themselves there was no dearth of critics, and the contempt of Westernized Jews towards their Russian and Polish brethren, however ambivalent, was palpable.[15] Surely some of the anti-Semitic and even racist rhetoric was internalized. Jewish immigrants were, in general photographic treatments of life and labour, occasionally dealt with sympathetically, or at least benignly, such as in the 'street scenes' and individual portraits of Lewis W. Hine.[16] Unlike Riis, Hine does not seem to have identified the 'sweatshop' as a distinctly Jewish invention. Interestingly, he was deeply moved by the plight of not only Jews, but also refugees such as Bohemians, Macedonians, Serbs and Greeks in the wake of the First World War. But there is little evidence that Hine's pictures had much resonance in the Jewish street; the dominant renderings of Jewry by both anti-Semites and well-intentioned liberal reformers bore little relation to the self-image in the Jews' own inner eye. This study aspires towards the reconstruction of that internal Jewish visual discourse, as it developed in the West, over a half-century. This is a period in which Jews have been seen primarily as in the throes of shedding their communal identity. Paula Hyman, in particular, has issued a clarion call to fellow historians to hold this paradigm up to closer scrutiny.[17] This project also seeks to engage ongoing debates in the humanities about what sense we can make of pictures, and how images function in constituting the public sphere. This study furthermore provides an opportunity to integrate Jewish history into these discussions, and to test their efficacy and limitations when confronted with a largely unacknowledged archive.[18] Such records of Jewish life deserve to be treated as something other than nostalgia or strewn wreckage.

Although the polemical and lobbying endeavours of Jewish 'defence' or 'self-defence' organizations against anti-Semitism are fairly well mined, there are comparatively few inquiries into the attempted construction of Jewish ethnic-political identities, by Jews themselves, through iconography and pictorial representations. Social historian Bill Williams observed in 1976 that 'If the place of "class" is well known, comparatively little attention has been devoted to the more autonomous groupings which centre upon nationality and religion.'[19] This may be seconded, with few objections, over twenty years later. Theoretical literature, as well as historical and sociological studies, tenaciously clings to this model. Surely, gender analysis has made great progress. There are occasional nods to ethnic differences and attempts to compensate for the excesses of imperialism and colonialism, which the rise of 'subaltern studies' has made some headway to ameliorate.[20] But few such works are based on primary-source historical evidence for the periods or subjects being elucidated.[21] The Jewish effort at 'regeneration' in a political and national sense need not be eschewed in the wake of stigmatization of Jews as 'degenerate'. Few scholars of modern Jewry have been moved by Lawrence W. Levine's assertion that 'Historians have the same obligations to their dead subjects that anthropologists have to their living ones. They must recognize their humanity, search for their points of view, respect their complexity. The dictum that "God is in the details" has particular relevance for historians. It is precisely the details that . . . photographs help us to recover.'[22] This study looks at Jews as creators and purveyors of culture, and as designers of their own paradigms in producing alternatives to the dominant discourse of politics and nation. Obviously Jews were, and in important respects remain, a fragmented community. So there always exist a multiplicity of discourses among Jews at any given time, divided as they are by regional variations within nations, Sephardi versus Ashkenazi origins, class distinctions, age cohorts, differences in attitude towards religious observance, and numerous other ways the group divides itself. But it is germane to talk about common Jewish perceptions, when one considers the dominance of the mass areas of Jewish settlement, particularly New York's Lower East Side and London's East End. Although Zionism, Yiddishism, Jewish socialism, territorialism, trade unionism, religious parties and other movements did not uniformly succeed in mastering the fate of their imagined constituencies, scholars need not be blind to their efforts to carve out Jewish public spaces. In the terms of nationalism scholar Anthony Smith, the representations evoked by these causes provide a kind of ethnic 'map'[23] that has rarely been consulted. And within the contemporaneous Jewish communities themselves, it is clear that such images contained various 'codes' for understanding Jewish politics and peoplehood.[24] Long before 'black is beautiful' became the watchword for African-American pride, Jews among themselves often spoke of the handsomeness of their leaders. The kind of good looks they praised as appropriate for their heroes was no simple aping of the Gentiles; the modern Jewish knight-errant could be unapologetically dark, wiry-haired and wearing spectacles – as was the case with Baruch Charney Vladeck when he entered the United States in 1908 (illus. 2). This was 'a real man'.[25] Melech Epstein, a commentator who was not prone to generosity, prefaced his profile of Chaim Zhitlovsky by asserting that 'Zhitlowsky was a handsome man with sparkling blue eyes and thick blond hair and beard. His appearance, plus his poise and academic bearing, made him an impressive figure.' After establishing his physical presence, the synopsis continues: 'A voluminous writer, a first-rate lecturer, and a witty and resourceful debater, who spiced his arguments with a fund of anecdotes, [Zhitlowsky had a] critical approach to the various party

2 Baruch Charney Vladeck (1886–1938): Exhibiting the characteristics that provided fodder for Marx's racist denunciations of Ferdinand Lassalle, Vladeck was compared to Lassalle in entirely positive terms. Photograph taken around the time of his arrival in America, from Vladeck, *Vladeck in lebn un shafen* (1936).

3 Chaim Zhitlovsky (1865–1943) (top left), surrounded by Morris Winchevsky (1856–1932), S. Janowsky (1864–1939), Isaac Hourwich (1860–1924) and Victor Tschernov (middle of right-hand column). Group portrait from a memorial volume published by the Arbeter Ring, from Hertz, *Fuftzig yor arbeter-ring* (1950).

doctrines [that] stimulated the thinking of many thousands in the United States and in Europe.'[26] Similar sentiments were echoed by a picture caption in a publication of the Arbeter Ring: 'Dr H. Zhitlovsky, socialist, revolutionary and preeminent Yiddish writer' (illus. 3, top left). About the towering figure in Hebrew and Yiddish literature, Y. L. Peretz, it was recalled that he was 'Of medium height, with broad shoulders and a large head . . . he carried himself like an aristocrat, impressing all who met him. He attracted a wide circle of both young and older writers and his home became a centre for Jewish radicals' (illus. 4).[27] Hence the physiognomy, stature and mind were conceived in total; a rhetoric of virility, of spawning ardent followers, seemed a natural consequence of the leaders' intellectual labour and charisma.

It may be argued that the aspect of Jewish politics that sought most deliberately to use the visual to its advantage was the Zionist movement, which released hundreds of multiply reproduced images

4 Y. L. Peretz (1851?–1915): A frequently reproduced image of a giant of Hebrew and Yiddish literature.

beginning in 1897. For the most part these have been used by scholars for narrowly illustrative purposes, but left unquestioned – in the spirit that Marc Bloch encourages historians to engage in a dialogue with their evidence.[28] Laurence Silberstein writes that one of the chief problems with contemporary Zionist scholarship is that historians (as well as their audiences) tend to see all representations of the movement, except those that are unmistakably 'literary', as having a one-to-one correspondence with 'reality'.[29] This observation may be applied to Jewish politics beyond Zionism. Obviously narratives and pictures do not simply describe, capture, or reproduce 'history'. A striking example of the instability of Zionist 'reality' is the multiple use of the image of Theodor Herzl looking over the Rhine Bridge in Basel (illus. 5, 6), Herzl's depiction in drawings as an Arab–Jewish warrior (illus. 7), and as Moses smashing the Ten Commandments (illus. 8). These super-manipulated images remind us that it is crucial 'to attend to the constituted rather than the found quality of seemingly "natural" phenomena',[30] as 'sight is shaped culturally and linguistically and that there is far more to seeing than meets the eye'.[31] In others words, besides telling a story, each picture has a history behind it and intersecting it, and the image itself may have been not only carefully staged and framed, but completely reformulated.

To be sure, a number of richly illustrated volumes using art and photography exist on aspects of Jewish history and culture. Yet those which broach a sustained, scholarly analysis, which are not primarily catalogues of exhibitions, are few.[32] Among the volumes on modern Jewry which have been attuned to the interplay of texts and images, and aware of the theoretical bases and implications of their studies, are Richard I. Cohen's *Jewish Icons*, John Efron's *Defenders of the Race*, James Young's *The Texture of Memory*, Steven Aschheim's *Brothers and Strangers* and Sander Gilman's *Kafka: The Jewish Patient*;[33] Jonathan Frankel makes excellent use of political cartoons in his magisterial *Prophecy and Politics*.[34] Nevertheless, many treatments of Jewish visual or popular culture do not touch on pertinent theoretical issues and, above all, reveal a reluctance to question the dissonance between the image and the subject. It has been stated as a historical axiom that 'all cultures require icons',[35] but the icons of Jewry at the end of the nineteenth century and in the first half of the twentieth century have barely been recovered, let alone interpreted. As opposed to a formalist analysis of Jewish iconography, my aim is to illuminate the historical processes that are accessible through Jews' public self-representation over a period of several decades, within Western communities in which they are recalled primarily for their efforts at acculturation within the majority culture.[36] In other words, it is in Eastern Europe and Palestine where Jews have been recognized for trying to mould their political identity. Here, though, I will explore the West, to look against the current of a supposedly overwhelming imperative towards acculturation.

The study that follows is based upon a selection of what I have determined to be representative photographic and graphic images that for the most part correspond to real persons and events.[37] Despite the fact that the images and even the memory of many of the figures to be considered here have been 'discarded', I wish to raise the spectre of their potency, especially as they 'rubbed harshly against the grain'[38] of both anti-Semitism and ultra-assimilationism.[39] In many cases these pictures recall an individual who was known also through appearances – and reports of appearances – at rallies and other public gatherings. Often their oratory as well as their writing distinguished their participation in Jewish politics. Taken even further, there is evidence of a specific corporeality attached to these people's pictures and words: a unique physical presence was often brought to mind as well. Among women Zionists in Britain, for instance, the fact that Rebecca Sieff was seen as 'brilliant and handsome' contributed to her ability to ignite 'the imagination of the rank and file of Jewish women';[40] another

5 Theodor Herzl (1860–1904): Herzl was photographed by the artist E. M. Lilien looking over the Rhine Bridge in Basel during the heady days of the First Zionist Congress. Herzl was thrilled with this picture.

memoirist writes that 'She became a legend in her own day for her regal beauty and personal charm; but it was her fiery spirit . . . that won for her a place in history' (illus. 9). The terms 'fiery' and 'restless',[41] almost always implying unambiguously positive traits, appear with great frequency no matter what the brand of Jewish politics. Assertiveness and charisma were not off-putting, although there was room for those who exemplified a more reticent dignity such as the anarchist S. Janowsky or Herzl's successor, David Wolffsohn (illus. 10, 11 lower right). Hermann Lilliput, a labour editor of the *Jewish Daily Forward*

6 Lilien's portrait of Herzl (illus. 5) was superimposed over other settings; this version, used for a Jewish National Fund stamp, was the next most common.

7 Lilien also imagined Herzl as a Bedouin sheikh wielding a blood-stained sword. Drawing from *Jüdischer Nationalkalendar* (1915–16).

8 Herzl as 'Moses smashing the tablets'. Herzl appears in several guises in Lilien's Bible illustrations. From Lilien, *Die Bibel* (n.d.).

9 Rebecca D. Sieff (1890–1966): Like Henrietta Szold, Sieff played a crucial role in rescuing and resettling child victims of the Nazis, and never shied away from challenging those in power. From *Who's Who in WIZO* (1970).

is another character who was well-remembered in three dimensions: 'Lilliput, who stood over six feet and had a crown of red hair, was known throughout the movement as a gentle warrior. He was capable of weeping over the injuries of a dog; but when he was arrested in Czarist Russia for revolutionary work, he attacked a police guard for abusing some of the weaker prisoners, and he fought until he was beaten into insensibility.'[42]

When one talks of the space in which Jewish political discourse was conducted, the model posed by Jurgen Habermas of an 'ideological template' where 'private people come together as a public' is particularly apt. All of the political bodies to be surveyed here were, in essence, voluntary associations. Moreover, all of the figures to be discussed were situated in a particular 'print' culture, which Benedict Anderson identifies with the rise of nationalism,[43] and typically they were 'viewed through the prism of symbols and mythologies of the community's heritage'.[44] Roland Barthes comments that a press photograph has a very different 'message' depending on whether it is in a right- or left-wing newspaper;[45] the same may be said for determining a picture's reception in the 'general' or 'Jewish' press. Given a Jewish social location, I seek to discern 'a "core" of ethnicity, as it has been transmitted in the historical record and as it shapes individual

10 David Wolffsohn (1856–1914): A much more significant and popular figure than has been recognized, Wolffsohn helped keep the movement from disintegrating after Herzl's death. Postcard.

experience', which resides in the '"myths, memories, values and symbols" of modern Jewry'.[46]

Although a number of overlapping Jewish subcultures will be considered here, the 'public sphere' is a useful tool in discussing communities defined not simply by religious birthright, but also by the journals, posters, meetings, stories and heroes that constituted their common culture.[47] Here Walter Benjamin's notion of an 'optical unconscious' is also central, as emergent streams of Jewish politics seemed to be influenced by both traditionally Jewish and anti-Semitic motifs.[48] Later theorists, such as Miriam Hansen, and Oskar Negt with Alexander Kluge, building on the work of Benjamin and Habermas, have incorporated within the notion of the public sphere 'experience . . . which mediates individual perception with social meaning, [and] conscious with unconscious processes', including 'concrete needs, conflicts, anxieties, memories, hopes, and fantasies', and specifically, the 'optical unconscious'.[49] Regarding images, Benjamin is possibly best recalled for asserting that 'in the age of mechanical reproduction' the mass-produced copy of an artistic work loses its 'aura'; yet he also noted, echoing Heinrich Heine, that salable commodities may radiate a 'magical aura'.[50] It is this latter sensation that approximates the contemporary reception of the images considered here. One might go so far as to say that they helped effect an enchantment of Jewish politics.

Although the current theoretical arsenal was not available to the people who produced and disseminated the body of images to be investigated, I would argue that their intentions are compatible with a 'picture-reception' orientation – as there was a decided self-consciousness involved in the making and spreading of such political imagery. 'The pictorial turn' actually happened in politics generally, and Jewish politics specifically, well before the current scholarly fascination with images and image-making.[51] In this regard, the work and rediscovery of Walter Benjamin and to a lesser extent Aby Warburg and Erwin Panofsky as critical interlocutors should not be surprising. Benjamin was, after all, fascinated by both Jewish mysticism and secular materiality. As Michael Steinberg notes, 'Benjamin teaches us to historicize in an expansive and enriching manner. His own historiographic practice extends the categories of experience available to the historical scholar as well as the investigative and interpretive strategies that can be employed.'[52] In no small part much of the current discussion about seeing images as historical matter turns on a re-reading of Panofsky, such as that by Michael Ann Holly and W.J.T. Mitchell, and a recontextualization of his work.[53] Panofsky, like Warburg an art historian, was a forerunner of interdisciplinary historical research through his practice of 'iconology'. 'Iconology' does not offer a singular formula for understanding a representational form 'as a statement of explicit meanings', but is geared to addressing 'the elusive underlying cultural principles of representation. Its implied direction involves discussing how meaning becomes expressed in a specific visual order . . . it asks . . . why certain images, attitudes, historical situations, and so forth have assumed one particular shape at one particular time.'[54] Warburg advised us to look at artistic creations not simply as 'products of their time' but possibly as attempts to scrape 'against the grain' of the spirit of the age.[55] His 'decoding of images', particularly of the Pueblo Indians of North America, were connected to his sensitivity, as a traditionally rooted German Jew, towards the plight of East European Jewry during and after the First World War.[56] Of all three it may be said that they insisted 'on historical practice based on the moral homage to the past in its actuality',[57] in opposition to what Benjamin termed 'historicism'. In his 'Theses on the Philosophy of History' Benjamin wrote that historicism 'contents itself with establishing a causal connection between various moments in history. But no fact that is a cause is for that very reason historical. It became historical posthumously, as it were, through events that may be separated from it by thousands of years. A historian who takes this as his point of departure stops telling the sequence of events like the beads of a rosary. Instead, he grasps the constellation from which his own era has formed with a definite earlier one. Thus he establishes a conception of the present as the "time of the now" which is shot through with chips of Messianic time.'[58]

Benjamin was probably less than judicious in seeing all scholars of culture as dry-as-dust 'historicists', employing a caricature of Ranke's motto of practising history as 'wie es eigentlich gewesen', which has come to be known in the English-speaking world as history 'as it really happened'.[59] However much he may have underappreciated the work of Ranke and others such as Jacob Burckhardt for their subtlety, Benjamin's admonition to scholars was nevertheless well taken, and to no small extent enjoined by Warburg and Panofsky as anti-antiquarians. Those Benjamin positively referred to as 'historical materialists' were urged to recognize 'the sign of a Messianic cessation of happening, or, put differently, a revolutionary chance in the fight for the oppressed past'. Such scholars were implored to take 'cognizance of it in order to blast a specific era out of the homogenous course of history – blasting a specific life out of the era or a specific work out of the lifework'.[60]

Messianism, or redemption on a cosmic scale, however, was not often touted openly in Jewish politics, except among the religious parties. But it certainly was subtly interwoven in nearly every Jewish political stream, in speeches, writings and pictures – in figures as diverse as Baruch Charney Vladeck (see illus. 2) and Gustav Landauer (see illus. 88). The evidence of messianic tremors is apparent in the response to specific media and events, particularly so by the writings of devotees of Theodor Herzl and Joseph Barondess. Gershom Scholem recognized that his receipt of a portrait of Herzl, as a childhood gift, was a galvanizing moment in his life.[61] Still, messianism hardly was discussed in the process of image-fabrication. Indeed, leaving aside the heady question of messianism, it is difficult to find ruminations on the image-making process itself – with Zionism being the notable exception. Zionists took pains to explain what their symbols were meant to mean, and even shared the process of their creation.[62] But in other arenas when this does surface, it is important to take note. In 1937, the *Handbook of Trade Union Methods* of the International Ladies' Garment Workers' Union advised its members to 'Think pictures first, for they are more important than news.' 'Many people', the guide continues, 'have difficulty in reading the printed word but read pictures easily. You can also get words across to readers in pictures that you could not get in the news columns.'[63] Hence it is clear that the image-makers in this organization were keenly aware that not only are pictures important, but that they may be more important than words, and that people read images differently than written texts.

Moreover, even though the International Ladies' Garment Workers' Union was not an expressly 'Jewish' organization, its heads were sensitive to the fact that it was perceived as 'Jewish'. Therefore they wanted to picture the 'national "types"' in its ranks positively.[64] We may assume that the 'national "types"' referred to are mainly Jewish. In the literature both supportive of and hostile to the trade union movement, an underlying assumption is that organized garment workers are mostly Jews and that their leadership is Jewish. In John Dyche's *Plea for Constructive Unionism* published in 1926, the author felt compelled to inform his readers that the book's anti-communist stance was not anti–Semitic.[65] Certainly, the author was right to infer that this would be a likely assumption. In one anti-Semitic and anti-trade union tirade of 1909, the stereotype of Jews as leaders and sympathizers of unionism and socialism is conflated with the (hyper-inflated) accusation that Jews possessed the monopoly on 'white slavery' – the international traffic in prostitutes, who may even be held captive against their will.[66] The anti-union tracts, which are not always figured into the matrix of anti-Semitism, suggest that discourses against which the varieties of Jewish politics asserted themselves operated on several levels. But there could be no doubt that anti-unionism of a certain sort was anti–Semitic, and that pro-unionism of a certain sort was a positive affirmation of Jewishness in the secular socio-political realm. In contrast to myriad unflattering allegations against self-organized Jewry, one of the most prominent shared features of the divergent positions was that Jews representing autonomously Jewish movements were morally upright, respectable and supremely dignified.

In addition to the compatibility of Jewish political image-making with theories concerning the interpretation of pictures, this study also lends itself to interrogating the historical location and function of the public sphere – allowing for the existence of alternate public spheres largely defined by the use of media. Very little of the stuff of Jewish politics pretended to hover 'above the marketplace' like national politics in the United States or parliamentary politics in Germany, France, or Britain.[67] Portraits of Zionist leaders Theodor Herzl and Max Nordau and postcards of the Zionist Congresses were always sold (see illus. 11); rarely were they given away, like ephemera in elections. Even utopian ideas were weighted down by the realization that media like newspapers and public meetings had to be paid for somehow, and that poets and writers had to make a living. Certainly there was selflessness and altruism as a motivating force for many, but one finds little sense of the new Jewish politics as a kind of gentlemen's club whose members did not have to concern themselves with daily life.

Although I do not wish to engage the debate over Jewish 'power' versus 'powerlessness', as exemplified by the controversy surrounding David Biale's *Power and Powerlessness in Jewish History*,[68] I proceed from the assumption that Jews did have some control, in the way of image-making and mediation, of the representation of their corporate aspirations and orientation to politics. It is widely acknowledged that Jews helped mould perceptions of themselves through the film industry; but the 'shaping of their public image' in other, less commercial ways has been largely unexplored.[69] 'One of the more illusive and difficult histor-ical truths', Lawrence W. Levine writes, 'is that even in the midst of disaster life goes on and human beings find ways not merely of adapting to forces that buffet them but often of rising above their circumstances and participating openly in the shaping of their lives.' Levine recalls Ralph Ellison's admonition to scholars concerning the study of African–Americans: 'Can a people . . . live and develop for over three hundred years just by reacting?'[70] But even in their films, wedded as they were to financial demands, Jews were able to rise beyond 'self-reflec-tion'.[71] In books and periodicals intended for popular audiences, explicit

11 This advertisement appeared on scores of occasions in German-language Zionist organs. Herzl, Wolffsohn and Max Nordau were clearly the movement's leading icons. The fact that the primary language of early Zionism was German made it accessible to Eastern Jews and 'respectable' to more modern established Western Jews.

portrayals of ennobled Jewish 'types' are particularly indicative of this motive, such as one finds in *Hakhme Yisrael ba-Amerika* by Benzion Eisenstadt;[72] *Kunstbaylage*, the weekend arts supplement of the *Forward* (beginning 1897);[73] the *Jüdischer Almanach* (1902, 1904, 1910) (illus. 12, 13) which was one of the early and most successful products of the Jüdischer Verlag;[74] 'Jüdische Kriegspostkarten' (Jewish war postcards of the First World War);[75] *Das ostjüdische Antlitz* [The East European Jewish Countenance] (1920, 1922) with text by Arnold Zweig and pictures by Hermann Struck;[76] the journal *Ost und West* (1901–23), edited by Leo Winz; *Des shpigel fun der ist sayd* [The Mirror of the East Side] (1923) by Jacob Magidoff;[77] *Photographs of the New Working Palestine* (1935) by Yaakov Benor-Kalter,[78] with numerous imitations; and pictures of Jewish sporting heroes, especially boxers. Theoretical models must in this instance be adapted to the construction of a decid-edly 'minority' discourse. As opposed to the efforts at illuminating 'the imposition of cultural homogeneity' and the hegemony of majority cultures,[79] the goal here is to explore a form of resistance to this 'imposi-tion' and urge towards conformity.

Rather than being dehumanized by 'publicity' and mass culture, which often is assumed to be an inescapable consequence of an increas-ingly media- and commodity-driven society,[80] the visual instruments of political mobilization seemed to be an effective means of realizing Jewish potential, which should not be treated as 'delusionary'.[81] By

12 Hermann Struck (1876–1944), *Polish Jew*. Though his creations outside of Zionism were relatively insignificant, Struck played a critical role in the incor-porating of Jewish themes into modern art, especially through his support of Marc Chagall. Etching, from *Jüdischer Almanach II* (1904).

13 Hermann Struck, *Sabbatausgang*. Another religious theme illustrated by Struck: the Havdalah ceremony. Etching, from *Jüdischer Almanach II* (1904).

participating in political movements Jews often sensed – correctly – that their efforts led to greater solidarity and progress.[82] As one cultural historian observes, 'it no longer seems tenable to try to establish strict correspondences between cultural cleavages and social hierarchies, creating simplistic relationships between particular cultural objects or forms and specific groups. On the contrary, it is necessary to recognize the fluid circulation and shared practices that cross social boundaries.'[83] With this in mind it is easier to grasp the admiration that Rose Schneiderman and others in the non-Zionist, working-class organizations held for the well-born (if not effete) Louis Brandeis (see illus. 77), appropriating him as a champion of Jews and other downtrodden workers.[84] Likewise those of a more 'radical' orientation, such as Isaac Hourwich (see illus. 3, bottom right) and Baruch Charney Vladeck, articulated and personified the necessity of building bridges to middle-class progressives in order to achieve the aims of Jewish labour.

As Negt and Kluge assert regarding working-class movements, there was a need for 'solidarity which could be grasped by the senses'.[85] Jewish labour organizers and socialists were at least as adamant as their non-Jewish counterparts in developing their own 'alternative culture'.[86] The power of the 'worker-photograph' was articulated by Willi Muenzenberg,[87] a 'founder of the Young Communist Movement' in Weimar Germany, who was also concerned with 'the structure

14 Nahum Sokolow (1859–1936): Shown at the Twelfth Zionist Congress (1921), Sokolow, like Wolffsohn, was seen as a moderating force in Zionism, especially when compared to the tempestuous Chaim Weizmann.

of photography'. 'Photography', Muenzenberg wrote in 1931, 'has become an outstanding and indispensable means of propaganda in the revolutionary class struggle.'[88] Indeed, Muenzenberg's own richly illustrated evening paper was reported to have 'a circulation of several hundred thousand, while the official [German Communist] daily, *Rote Fahne*, had less than 40,000.'[89] But Zionism, which deliberately sought to bridge class divisions, also exhibited this sensual-sensitive urge, particularly with regard to illustrating the 'new Jewish life' in Palestine. Furthermore, the movement sought to merge sight with sound in promoting its message. Zionist leaders such as Nahum Sokolow (illus. 14) and Siddy Wronsky were known for their appearances in public forums, but also through the phonograph recordings they made for the cause, which were distributed by the Jewish National Fund, a chief fundraising arm of the movement before 1921. Similarly, the countenance of Morris Winchevsky would have been known not only to the devotees of his writings and poetry in London and New York, where he spent fifteen and thirty-eight years, respectively, but 'his poems were sung in the tenement shops of New York,

15 Another version of the picture of Morris Winchevsky that appeared in the Arbeter Ring volume (illus. 3). Winchevsky was the backbone of Yiddish journalism in London before he went to America.

Boston, Chicago, London, and Manchester . . .' (illus. 15; see also illus. 3, upper right).⁹⁰ Winchevsky's points of reference included Leicester and London, such as in his song 'Dray Shvester' (Three Sisters), a lament on the conditions of the Jewish poor. Many of his lyrics, however, stressed the brotherhood of Jewish workers and aspired to lift their spirits.⁹¹

Although many of these names faded in Jewish memory after a single generation, they recall individuals who figured prominently in the visualization of Jewish politics in the first half of the twentieth century. I have therefore limited the scope here to images that were published and disseminated for the purpose of reaching an audience beyond an individual's friends, professional cohort and family; I have attempted to choose from those images that were intended for the Jewish public at large, and signify 'shared'⁹² rather than idiosyncratic ideologies. As such these 'are not merely reflective' of modern Western Jewry; they played some part in influencing 'people's thought and behaviour', and therefore may be considered both 'document and historical force in one'.⁹³ In this regard I take it for granted that visual and verbal media – sights, sounds and other impressions – incessantly interact, as 'all media' are inherently layered, or 'mixed media'.[94]

It is important to recognize that even realistic images 'are constructed for the purpose of performing some function within a given sociocultural matrix'.[95] John Tagg asserts that '*every* photograph is the result of specific and, in every sense, significant distortions which render its relation to any prior reality deeply problematic . . .'[96] Although 'photographic images, like statistics, do not lie . . . the truths they communicate are elusive and incomplete'.[97] Further, 'they are filled with contractions and paradoxes, as the most valuable historical sources frequently are'.[98] I seek, therefore, to determine 'the functions of imagery' within their specific milieu, to explore 'what images were (and are) made to mean on the basis of how they were (and are) used'.[99] The most immediate 'possibilities of meaning'[100] for the Jewish audience are the main points of reference. Added to the problem of determining the meaning of specific images are questions such as: who constituted the intended audience? What was the result of their encounter with the subject? And how did this very encounter shape the impact of the phenomenon? As my approach is historical, I am mainly concerned with investigating the transitions of Jewish politics and Jewry from 1881 to 1939, as well as determining the consequences of these changes.

It is crucial, as well, to affirm that 'viewers are active participants in determining meaning',[101] and that 'spectators' and/or an audience are not a spongy mass. Why and how one becomes a spectator may be a factor of one's sex, class, generation, ethnic-national subgroup, or any number of other factors.[102] In addition to recognizing distinct national-Jewish contingents and differences between Ashkenazim and Sephardim, it is true as well that Jews identified with different sects of Judaism and degrees of disassociation with institutional Judaism. Despite the fact that an image or text's precise reception is notoriously difficult to gauge, I have attempted to examine the images and the ways they were received when they were deployed. In part, this is an attempt to reclaim the response to the media.[103] It is from the perspective of spectatorship that women's roles take on a heightened importance. It is interesting that Miriam Hansen begins her study of *Spectatorship in American Silent Film* with the 1897 premiere of 'The Corbett–Fitzsimmons Fight', noting that women made up a substantial share of the audience. 'Unlike live prizefights with their all-male clientele', Hansen writes, 'the cinematic mediation of the event gave women access to a spectacle from which they traditionally had been excluded.'[104] Although I do not wish to exaggerate the overwrought analogy between sport and politics-as-a-game, it does not seem accidental that women became notable 'spectators' in Jewish politics, particularly Zionism, beginning in the summer of 1897 with the First Basel Congress. Perhaps this was true for the founding of the Jewish Socialist Party in New York, also in 1897. The situation in the Basel Stadtcasino was, however, quite unlike the one-way reception of the filmed prizefight (an audience watching a film in a theatre). In the case of women watching male Zionists from the gallery in Basel, the men attending the Congress were reciprocally titillated, as their manly performance happened before a throng of appreciative ladies.[105]

The notion of Zionist and Jewish trade union leaders having a seductive quality was not totally hidden in accounts of the movement, in which notions of eroticism and messianism were intertwined.[106] Above all this was true of Theodor Herzl, the founder of 'political' Zionism.[107] But the early Jewish labour movement in New York also boasted an 'unselfish and courageous' champion who possessed a strikingly handsome Semitic countenance. In Edward King's fictionalized account of the life of the leader of the Cloakmakers' Union, Joseph Barondess (illus. 16), Zalmonah (the Barondess figure) is a veritable heart-throb. Tall and alluring, with 'blue fearless eyes' and a brow 'marked with power', he was a magnet to beautiful women.[108] In union meetings he was 'worshipped by the mothers and wives who recognized in him the deliverer, leading their sons and husbands up out of the land of Egypt . . .'[109] Interestingly, both Barondess and Herzl had theatrical aspirations: Herzl as a playwright, and Barondess as an actor.[110] In a reminiscence about the diverse attributes of Sidney Hillman that contributed to his effective leadership – including *yiches* (prestigious, notably learned forebears), talmudic acumen and broad humanism – Rose Schneiderman made sure to include his attractiveness to women (illus. 17 and 18, top left):

I first met Sidney in 1913 when he visited the needle-trades union in New York, the year before he came there to help the Cloakmakers set up a system to take care of the needs of its huge membership, which had grown tremendously since their general strike in 1910. We met at a beach picnic on Staten Island organized by mutual friends and, from that time on, we were good friends. Sidney was quite a charmer and several of the girls there were prepared to fall in love with him but he was already engaged to Bessie Abramowitz . . . Sidney was a slender young man, then in his middle twenties. He was entirely wrapped up in trade unionism, as we all were. That was all we talked about in those days and that's what we talked about that Sunday on Staten Island. And, of course, the future of mankind. I remember how very gay and witty Sidney was and I knew even then that he had the ability to get along with people . . . Sidney was a Talmudic scholar, a descendant of a long line of learned rabbis, but he had rebelled against his father's choice of a

16 Joseph Barondess (1867–1928): Barondess's life was seen as a classic rags-to-riches story; he was the outstanding charismatic figure of the early trade union movement. Drawing by S. Raskin, from Magidoff, *Des shpigel fun der ist sayd* (1923).

career for him as a respectable rabbi. Coming to this country by way of England, he stopped first in New York, but after a short time moved on to Chicago where he learned to be a cutter at the Hart Schaffner & Marx factory and where he continued his intense interest in the plight of the worker which had first been aroused in his native land.[111]

Despite the fact that neither Zionism nor Jewish trade unionism was genuinely welcoming to women, spectatorship often evolved into recruitment. Throughout the interwar years the largest single segment of United States Zionists was Hadassah, the Women's Zionist Organization of America, and the International Ladies' Garment Workers' Union became a mainstay of the labour movement. 'Recruitment' also was often synonymous with the cultivation of fund-raising subscriptions and membership fees,[112] without which few of these organizations could have hoped to survive.

The point may indeed be argued that prominent women and women's organizations existed in the Jewish public realm to a greater degree than scholars have suggested. For example, one finds no women included in the authoritative anthologies of Zionism by Arthur Hertzberg and Shlomo Avineri,[113] or in older, collective portraits of

17 Sidney Hillman (1876–1946): A dashing young man in 1908. From Soule, *Sidney Hillman* (1939).

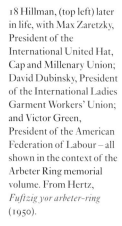

18 Hillman, (top left) later in life, with Max Zaretzky, President of the International United Hat, Cap and Millenary Union; David Dubinsky, President of the International Ladies Garment Workers' Union; and Victor Green, President of the American Federation of Labour – all shown in the context of the Arbeter Ring memorial volume. From Hertz, *Fuftzig yor arbeter-ring* (1950).

מ. הילמאן, פרעזידענט פון אמאלגאמייטעד קלאר־ וואירקערס יוניאן —

זאקס זאריצקי, פרעזידענט פון דער אינטערנעשאנעל יוניטער האט, קעפ און מילינערי יוניאן.

the Lower East Side of New York, such as *Profiles of Eleven* by Melech Epstein and *Des shpigel fun der ist seyd* by Jacob Magidoff.[114] Despite the title of his magnum opus that implies the contrary – *World of Our Fathers* – Irving Howe, on the other hand, shows that Jewish women played substantial roles, on many levels, in the Lower East Side. In Zionism during the interwar years Henrietta Szold was a dominant, if embattled leader. Before her ascendance to the head of Hadassah she was an important, if undervalued shaper of the programme and products of the Jewish Publication Society of America.[115] In New York's Lower East Side, certainly Lillian Wald and Rose Schneiderman deserve mention for their influence among the masses. Wald, 'the nurse who founded the Henry Street Settlement, grew within her lifetime into a figure of legend, known and adored on every street'.[116] Schneiderman was among the most critical interlocutors bringing the concerns of Jewish labour to the door of the Roosevelt White House, receiving a fair hearing, and ultimately a sincere embrace. Bertha Pappenheim and Siddy Wronsky spoke to the particular concerns of German-speaking Jewish women. The inclusion of women as spectators and main subjects in this study is not simply an attempt to detail their contributions,[117] but to refashion a narrative of Jewish history with notable women, as well as those of the rank and file, integrated into the whole. The history of movements such as Zionism and trade unionism, although clearly male-dominated, appear very different from the normative narratives when the history of women is deliberately and consistently interwoven.[118]

In addition to the consideration of women in Zionism, as opposed to the concentration on the male 'mainstream' which characterizes most Zionist historiography, mention should also be made of right-wing Revisionist Zionism. Images of Vladimir (Ze'ev) Jabotinsky (illus. 19) and Josef Trumpeldor (illus. 20) were significant icons of the movement, particularly in the Irish and South African Jewish communities.[119] As early as the 1920s, with the exception of the Revisionists' formal (but temporary) splintering from the World Zionist Organization, Zionism pursued a policy of greater inclusiveness, especially because fundraising became the organizational thrust of the movement. By the mid-1940s, as the facts of the Holocaust

19 Vladimir Jabotinsky (1880–1940): As leader of the right-wing Revisionist Zionists, Jabotinsky encountered a variety of responses; people hailed him as a saviour or pelted him with eggs and rotten fruit.

20 Josef Trumpeldor (1880–1929): An icon in Palestine and Eastern Europe, this one-armed pioneer's legend was not as widely known in the West.

were becoming known, and the Yishuv seemed to be endangered, the formerly harsh divisions between left, right and centre varieties of Zionism became obscured outside Palestine. A Jewish consensus was emerging in the West, which increasingly concurred that all and any means should be utilized to preserve the Jewish gains in Palestine, and to assure its viability as a refuge for world Jewry. Towards this end, the French prime minister Leon Blum was inspired to found the 'Socialist Committee for Palestine' in 1938, as ten years earlier he had participated in the inaugural meeting of the enlarged Jewish Agency in Zurich.

Along with the Zionist movement the images related to the Jewish workers' and trade union activities, 'Jewish' socialism and communism, territorialism, the political dimension of 'progressive' religious sects, and Orthodox and ultra-Orthodox parties are considered here. These varieties of Jewish politics may be defined against each other, and seen as along a spectrum of greater to lesser resistance to the established order, as well as greater to lesser rejection of an urge towards acculturation (in the majority society) which appeared to shun a distinctive Jewish identity. Beginning with the more explicitly radical orientation, I include the pictures disseminated in the Yiddish-communist press, under the direction of the chief icon of the far left, M. Olgin (illus. 21).

The kingmaker of the Jewish street for over half a century, however, was the editor of the *Forward*, Abraham Cahan (illus. 22, top right); he must be considered in light of his role in political myth making. Cahan is a quintessential figure in this study, because he stood in the realms of culture and politics, and his likeness could be used to promote politics from a specifically Jewish-leftist militancy, to Zionism, to 'assimilationism'. Hutchins Hapgood wrote that 'the great passion of the intellectual quarter results in the consciously held and warmly felt principle that literature should be a transcript from life. Cahan represents this feeling in its purest aspect; and he therefore is highly interesting not only as a man but as a type.'[120] Cahan shows that the lines between journalism and politics, and even poetry and politics, were almost always obscured in this period. Along with his novels and newspaper work, Cahan was revered as 'an eloquent and impassioned speaker'.[121]

Although Cahan was in a class of his own as the personification of a newspaper (in his case, the *Forward*), other papers, as well, were closely identified with their main moving spirits. Part of this is to do with the fact that most newspapers were forced to have public fundraising functions in order to carry on, and their editors and featured writers were the main speakers. Even the anarchists were pressed into this: 'The weekly Anarchistic paper, the *Fraye arbeter-shtimme*, prints about 7,000 copies. Of this circulation, with the assistance of balls, entertainments and benefits at the theatres, the paper is able to exist. It pays a

21 Moissaye Olgin (1874–1939): One of the political giants of his time and fervently dedicated to Yiddish culture, Olgin was nearly forgotten in America and his beloved Soviet Union. Cover of Kurtz, *Moshe Olgin* (1940).

salary to only one man, the editor S. Janowsky [see illus. 3, middle right and illus. 89], who receives the sum of $13 a week.'[122] Like so many of the figures of Jewish politics who wrote in different languages and advocated different programmes at various stages of their lives, the writer David Pinsky (illus. 23) and poets Abraham Reisen, Abraham Liesin and Morris Winchevsky also were 'transitional' figures. Pinsky, notes Hapgood, 'a writer for the *Abendblatt*, is very interesting not only as a writer of short sketches of literary value . . . but also as a dramatic critic and as one of the more wide-awake and distinctively modern of the young men of Yiddish New York'.[123] Winchevsky, like many of the others, 'is a Socialist, a man who has edited more than one Yiddish publication with success, of uncommon learning and cultivation'.[124] Both Shalom Aleichem (illus. 24) and Chaim Zhitlovsky (illus. 25) are remembered mostly for their contributions to Yiddish literature and the advocacy of a public space for Yiddishism, respectively; these men embodied what are generally considered contradictory aspects of Jewish–national politics at different times. The point I wish to stress, though, is that the Jewish element tended to overwhelm the specific political programme of the sect or individual.

The pantheon of Jewish politicos featured those aligned with socialism and trade unionism, such as Manny Shinwell (illus. 26) and Harold Laski in Britain, and Meyer London (see illus. 22, lower left), Rose Schneiderman and Morris Hillquit (see illus. 22, lower right), who were familiar to the Jewish masses of the Lower East Side. Baruch Charney Vladeck (see illus. 2), identified with the *Forward*, the Arbeter Ring and the United Hebrew Trades, also belongs with the affirmatively Jewish cohort of the pre-Second World War period. Vladeck, too, was at least as much a poet as a politico. Occasionally there were individuals of great importance, with thousands in their retinue, such as Joseph Barondess, who shunned affiliation with what he saw as political extremism. Barondess especially wished to distance himself from official leftist parties. The great scholar-agitator on the Lower East Side was Isaac Hourwich (see illus. 3, bottom right) who at one time lectured in economics and statistics at the University of Chicago. Along with personalities, organizations such as the Arbeter Ring, the United Hebrew Trades and the Jewish Section of the Socialist Labour Party became well-defined, vibrant elements of Jewish political life. Yet as opposed to the Zionist movement, which helped its constituents visualize a total Jewish society in Palestine, the purview of the occupation-based organizations was more circumscribed: the workmen's organizations mainly heralded their efforts at caring for members in sickness, duress and death.[125] Especially in the sphere of Jewish

22 There probably was no one in the world of American Jewish journalism who could compare in influence with Abraham Cahan (1860–1951), pictured here with Meyer London (1871–1926), Morris Hillquit (1869–1933) and Eugene Debs (1855-1926), the famous non-Jewish socialist. From Hertz, *Fufizig yor arbeter-ring* (1950).

23 David Pinsky (1872–1959): Representative of a group of dashing, dignified and cultivated modern writers. From *Kinder Tshurnal* (May 1947).

עניש אויפ'ן מארגן.   דער מארגן, אויף וויפיר זיי ביינ'
אך אים, ליגט פאר זיי אין דעם גאנץ גרויען עבר.

24 Shalom Aleichem (1859–1916): Shown here in the context of a Communist magazine, Aleichem was perhaps the most influential Yiddish writer and was appropriated by every wing of Jewish politics. From *Der Hamer* (May 1926).

25 Chaim Zhitlovsky in an official portrait later in life.

26 Manny Shinwell (1884–1986): Here looking almost meek, Shinwell was known for his feistiness, especially in the restrained world of British politics.

women, Jewish social welfare – for the purpose of uplifting Jewish women and tending to their needs – was personified by Siddy Wronsky and Bertha Pappenheim in Central Europe and Lillian Wald in the United States. In the Zionist milieu, perhaps the most dynamic mediator between Palestine and the United States was Henrietta Szold (illus. 27), and WIZO was a highly visible dimension of the British connection with Palestine.

Contrary to the popular belief that ultra-Orthodox Jewry abhorred any type of 'graven image',[126] anti-Zionist orthodox parties – particularly Agudas Yisroel – also had their own lionized leaders, such as Nathan Birnbaum,[127] R. Moshe Blau (illus. 28), R. Yosef Haim Sonnenfeld and Jacob Israel De Haan (illus. 29). These icons carried

27 Henrietta Szold's small size belied her toughness.

profound significance in Jewish circles, which are often incorrectly perceived as being hostile to the instruments of mass politics; this was not simply a matter of glorifying great rabbis.[128] De Haan, as the first victim of a Zionist 'political murder' in 1924, became a uniquely significant visage whose legacy continues to burn brightly in the world of the Haredim, or ultra-ultra-Orthodox (illus. 29). There also were progressive Jewish religious leaders, such as Moses Gaster (illus. 30), Stephen S. Wise (illus. 31) and Leo Baeck (illus. 32), whose poses embodied expressly political stances. Gaster was seriously considered as a successor to Theodor Herzl to lead world Zionism after Herzl's death in 1904. He is remembered now, however, more for the friction surrounding his Zionist career.[129]

Photographs and reproductions of portraits also were embossed

28 Rabbi Moshe Blau, an important Haredi anti-Zionist leader, was a significant figure inside and outside of Palestine.

29 Jacob Israel De Haan (1881–1924): One of the more bizarre and enigmatic personalities in Jewish history, De Haan seemed to embody irreconcilable contradictions.

30 Rabbi Moses Gaster (1856–1939): The 'Haham' of the London Sephardic community was one of the impressive, cultured rabbis at the early Zionist Congresses. From *Die Welt*, 19 November 1897.

31 Stephen S. Wise (1874–1949): Wise, shown here in a photograph by Halsman, was a crucial figure in the transformation of American Jewry in the first half of the 20th century.

32 Leo Baeck (1873–1956): His influence extended beyond Germany.

33 Lord Balfour was seen as a guiding force who would guarantee the promise of his Declaration and the Mandate for Palestine.

34 Max Nordau was a huge celebrity at the turn of the century. Tragically, his notion of 'degeneration' was largely absorbed into anti-Semitism.

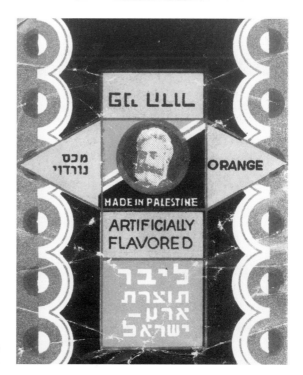

35 Nahum Sokolow being used to sell unsweetened condensed milk.

36 Eleanor Roosevelt doing her bit for Zionist fundraising.

'ephemera' which conveyed images of Jewish politics. Therefore, items intended for children, candy-wrappers bearing the images of Lord Balfour (illus. 33), Menahem Ussischkin and Max Nordau (illus. 34), a tobacco pouch sporting a portrait of Theodor Herzl, and milk-can labels showing Nahum Sokolow (illus. 35) and Herzl also inform the visual sensibility of Jewish politics. Lord Balfour, incidentally, is one of a handful of non-Jews who were perceived as operating in the Jewish fold or for specific Jewish interests. In a different quarter of Anglo-Jewry, another non-Jew was revered as a leading light: Rudolf Rocker, a radical socialist and trade union leader, who mastered the Yiddish of Whitechapel. Nor did George Washington, Tomáš Masaryk, Winston Churchill, Eugene Debs, Franklin Roosevelt and Eleanor Roosevelt (illus. 36), icons of continuing significance, avoid appropriation in Jewish politics. The Workmen's Circle, in 1935 'the largest and wealthiest immigrant labour fraternal order, as well as the largest Jewish organization in America', boasted that it was 'by no means an exclusively Jewish organization. One of its most prominent members is Norman Thomas, who is neither of the seed of Abraham nor of the creed of Moses.'[130] Leaving aside the issue of his disputed 'Jewishness', Christopher Columbus found his way into Jewish politi-cal discourse.[131] But no celebrity, Jewish or non-Jewish, had the cachet of Albert Einstein, a Zionist icon whose value to Jewish pride and nationalization was beyond compare (illus. 37).

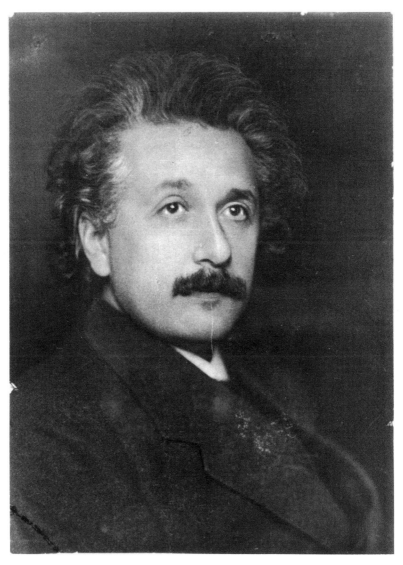

37 Albert Einstein (1879–1955): The face of genius and of an assertive Jewish national politics.

It may be argued that iconography became a means of entry to modern political movements and institutions, as well as a means to preserve, adapt and enchant forms of Jewish distinctiveness. In some respects the dominant (non-Jewish) paradigm of 'the other' and 'cosmopolitan' versus the 'authentic' and 'national' were turned on their heads. Diverse modes of Jewish political expression within national contingents, which have tended to be treated on their own terms – whether they be socialist, Zionist, Yiddishist, territorialist, religious,

49

liberal, or communist – deserve to be examined in light of each other. By the 1930s, there was a significant convergence among formerly competing, rigid divisions. The politics of both lower-class solidarity and expressly assimilationist agendas, among Jews, shifted into a vicarious support for Zionism, which was spearheaded by its 'Labour' faction.[132] A leftist stalwart in London asserted that the spirit of the old anarchist and trade unionist comrades was 'poured into the new movement which has established the State of Israel'.[133] One of the striking examples of this convergence may be found in the 1928 Jubilee volume of the *Gewerkschaften* of the United Hebrew Trades: despite the fact that he was the living exponent of 'Hebrew' labour, David Ben-Gurion conveyed his greetings, in Yiddish, to the union's rank and file.[134] The official history of the United Hebrew Trades ten years later would call the 'Histadruth', the federation of Zionist unions in Palestine, one of its 'kindred movements abroad', and it would increasingly dedicate itself to 'refugee aid work' and 'the development of Palestine as a homeland'.[135] Although it would be too glib to say that the political energies of American Jewry in the *Landsmannshaften* ('Old Country' home-town associations)[136] were reshaped to fit the drive for a Jewish 'homeland' from the turn of the century to 1939, the relationships between the political symbolism and strategies of apparently disparate movements do need to be rethought.

There were important elements of these groups which engendered explicit or implicit affinities. They usually favoured some type of co-operativism instead of unbridled competition; they sought the approval of the non-Jewish world; they had a more or less materialist *Weltanschauung*, maintaining that the world and politics worked according to observable, rational principles; they affirmed that Jewish men were the embodiment of manliness, and stood up against the 'insulted manhood' of the Jews;[137] they asserted that there was a positive value in Jews continuing to socialize among themselves, and conducting their cultural and political lives with a consciousness of their Jewishness; they also assumed that, whatever the form of the greater society, a recognizable Jewish subculture would and should continue to exist, which actively aspired to enhance the spiritual lives of its members. In sum, Jewry sought to escape from the bondage of irrational hatred through its organizational strategies, so that they would no longer be subject to the tyranny of entrenched economic and political interests. They would then be liberated, as Jews, to contemplate the universe and make their way with a free and fearless look. This typically assumed a penchant for bolstering one's cause with theoretical rationales, compared with the more simple, 'pragmatic' approach in much of political life. Perhaps this is no better illustrated than in the depiction of the 1914 debate between Samuel Gompers and Morris Hillquit by Carl Degler in *Out of Our Past*. Degler wishes to show the inferiority of Hillquit by contrasting the 'highly philosophical and theoretical aims of the Socialists' with 'the stubbornly unphilosophical, practical spirit of the Federation's eminent leader', Gompers.[138] It is possible to interpret Gompers's anti-philosophical stance as an indication of his desire to transcend Jewish concerns.

The Jewish politics that were vocationally and class-based, then, were able to meld with the more expressly ethnic and political forms of Jewish politics, as class and language affiliation no longer bound Jews in the same way. The visualization of Jewish politics helped make this possible. Hence Jews who were not previously enamoured of Zionism could find themselves in its orbit by the late 1930s. Furthermore, in that the Jewish settlement in Palestine was being led by the progressive-labour element in its midst, it was possible to transfer one's class loyalty to the dominant group in Zionism. Indeed, Zionism had long been equipped to recruit and sustain members for whom their tie to the movement was experienced vicariously.

A central argument in this study, then, is similar to that of Eli Lederhendler in *The Road to Modern Jewish Politics*, which concerns East European Jewry in the nineteenth century, before the watershed date of 1881. Lederhendler contends that a full-blown Jewish politics did not simply erupt in the wake of the pogroms. He argues that many of the mechanisms were soundly in place before the pogroms of 1881 and the ensuing tremors brought them to the surface.[139] I believe that one may adopt a similar view of Jewish politics, vis-à-vis Zionism, after 1947–8. Although I do not mean to minimize the significance of the Holocaust and the birth of the State of Israel, I contend that a great deal of the infrastructure in the Western Jews' minds' eye, and even finished products of Jewish politics, were in a process of mobilization by the time of the Second World War and the Holocaust. As Jews became less working-class and Yiddish-speaking, and as their status was threatened in Central Europe, Zionism was left as one of the more viable alternatives for an affirmatively Jewish, moderately politicized form of self-identification. And it was a phenomenon they had been trained to 'see'. Regarding the United States in the 1930s, Warren Sussman has written that photography, radio and film 'created a special community of all Americans (possibly an international community) unthinkable previously. The shift to a culture of sight and sound was of profound importance; it increased our self-awareness as a culture; it helped create a unity of response and action not previously possible; it made us more susceptible than ever to those who would mold culture and thought.'[140] Within the dominant, macro-cultures of the Americans, British, French, Germans, Dutch and others resided a variety of Jewish micro-cultures that simultaneously resisted and absorbed the larger trends, and built up worlds of their own. A critic of the visual arts writes that 'The more fragile our identity, the more we need to reinforce it. To show that we exist.'[141] Beyond asserting the mere existence of Jewry as a whole and its corporate bodies, the men and women behind these images fervently sought the transformation of themselves and their world into something greater. 'We know', wrote Walter Benjamin at the conclusion of his 'Theses on the Philosophy of History' (XVIII B), 'that the Jews were prohibited from investigating the future. The Torah and the prayers instruct them in remembrance, however. This stripped the future of its magic, to which all those succumb who turn to soothsayers for enlightenment. This does not imply, however, that for the Jews the future turned into homogeneous, empty time. For every second of time was the strait gate through which the Messiah might enter.'[142] Messianism, for Western Jews in the early twentieth century, would assume any number of guises; its pace and form depended on the particular strains of Jewish politics with which one identified. Such hopes were stirred not only from religious traditions and modern ideologies, but through the engagement of specific Jewish countenances.

2 The Gallery of Zionists

Numerous politicized groups of Western Jews from the late nineteenth century onwards deployed symbols and images, and attempted to muster their forces with pictures of their heroes. Zionism, however, was the Jewish movement *par excellence*, which sought to influence its constituents with portrayals of its leadership and its movement in action. In his voluminous diaries, Zionism's founder, Theodor Herzl, made clear his intention to mobilize the Jews in the same manner that other nations came to be galvanized – with banners, ribbons and flags – and by positively exploiting his people's collective fantasies.[1] He also recognized the growing power of his own legend as well as the charismatic attraction of his chief lieutenant in Zionism, Max Nordau.[2] To the extent that Herzl and his cohort partially succeeded at 'conquering' the Jewish communities,[3] this was achieved in no small measure by lionizing his movement's leaders, the most significant of whom was himself.

Their message was also conveyed through the evolving spectacle of Zionism's chief institution, its Congress, in which its leaders were embedded (illus. 38). The Congress was an unprecedented pseudo-parliamentary body in the Jewish world; the attempt to secure a Jewish homeland in Palestine was, of course, the focus of the movement's politics. Zionists, furthermore, vividly showcased the new Jewish life that was taking root in Palestine. The movement's media featured the 'New Jews' who were nurturing, and themselves being nurtured, by the revived Promised Land (illus. 39). Zionism's concern with documenting and illustrating the productiveness of the Jews in Palestine was similar to other groups' attempts to show that Jewry under their auspices was eminently productive, as opposed to having a parasitic relationship with the general economic order. This discourse originated in the debates about Jewish emancipation in the eighteenth century. It is not surprising, then, that the United Hebrew Trades in the United States, the various territorialist movements and the Alliance Israélite Universelle in France enshrined productivization, too, as a main hallmark.

38 The combination of the dignified setting and the participants' tremendous enthusiasm made striking spectacles of the early Zionist Congresses. Photograph by Emil Buri printed on a postcard.

To be sure, Zionism was a minority movement within a minority, and an embattled one at that. Compared with alternatives for immigration, Palestine was not the people's choice, despite the fact that it obviously became an important locus of Jewish settlement, particularly in the years between the wars, and during and after the Holocaust. What most concerns us here, however, is how Zionism became a factor of Jewish identity outside Eastern Europe and Palestine. In dwelling on these Zionist-disseminated images I do not wish to suggest that a majority of Western Jews called themselves Zionists. It seems, however, that Zionism had a disproportionately large impact on the self-image of modern Jews, affecting even those who were only mildly interested in or indifferent to its aims. One did not have to be a Zionist to have been regularly exposed to Zionist media, and throughout the West Zionist politics came to be more and more intermingled with formerly anti-Zionist bodies ranging from trade unions to rabbinical seminaries.[4] Hence, Zionism's share in comprising the self-image of Western Jews loomed larger than its limited, if not paltry, membership rolls.

Simply put, Theodor Herzl is the most significant Jewish icon of modern times. One of his most astute biographers, Ernst Pawel, has written that Herzl was the first and the greatest modern Jewish leader. Little wonder that Herzl's countenance, more than any other, came to

קרן קימת לישראל

גאולה
תתנו לארץ

לשנה טובה תכתבו ותחתמו

39 Hundreds of depictions of Jewish agriculture stressing that Jews were rebuilding the Land of Israel through their own labour were disseminated by the Zionist organization. New Year's greetings postcard from the Jewish National Fund.

epitomize Jewish political aspirations during the fin-de-siècle. Even for non-Zionists, it was possible to exalt him, as did Sigmund Freud, as a champion of 'the human rights' of the Jews.[5] The exhilaration generated by Herzl's physical presence during his brief tenure at the head of Zionism, and reproductions of his photographed, drawn, painted and sculpted torso – which were ubiquitous as from 1897 – provided a figure above all others in the Jews' national self-imagination. Herzl embodied simultaneously a cultured Viennese, a dignified European statesman and the ideal new man that Zionism aspired to create. That he also was seen as a messianic incarnation is beginning to be explored by historians;[6] during Herzl's own time, this was part of the case waged against him by the Orthodox establishment.

The First Zionist Congress, or Basel Congress, of 1897 was equivalent to a seismic eruption in the Jewish political landscape, which exceeded all expectations in garnering notoriety and visibility for the Zionist cause. The impact of the perception of Herzl at the Congress was detailed time and again. Upon seeing Herzl at the dais a delegate reported:

It is no longer the elegant Dr Herzl of Vienna; it is a royal scion of the House of David, risen from among the dead, clothed in legend and fantasy and beauty. Everyone sat breathless, as if in the presence of a miracle . . . The dream of two thousand years was on the point of realization; it was as if the Messiah, son of David, confronted us; and I was seized by an overpowering desire, in the midst of this storm of joy, to cry out, loudly, for all to hear: "Yehi hamelech!" Hail to the King![7]

During the six Zionist Congresses over which he presided, and the mass meetings he addressed in London, Vienna and elsewhere, thousands of Zionists gazed upon Herzl's face. Others came to know him not only through his speeches and writings and reportage of his

Zionist activity, but by scores of pictures that circulated throughout the Jewish world. That these pictures, especially in the form of post-cards, were in transit before being framed or tacked up on walls should not be taken as evidence that they were trivial. On the contrary, the fact that these often changed hands, and that the same picture was present in different locales, is significant. Due to the international nature of its constituency and global aspirations, Zionism's images proved to be decisive among the unifying forces of modern Jewry. Although it is too simple to say that Herzl's image was the pre-eminent bond of Jewish solidarity, the power of his countenance, in the service of Zionist nationalization, was remarkable. Herzl's picture helped Jews imagine themselves as members of a vaguely defined, yet emerging Jewish nation – no matter where they lived.

The most popular image of Herzl was the etching by Hermann Struck of the early 1900s. Jacob De Haas, a hagiographer of Herzl, identifies the picture as a 'painting' that was 'generally referred to as "The Last Phase"' (illus. 40).[8] This picture was copied, sometimes accurately, sometimes grossly, in scores of settings. For example, it appeared in

40 Hermann Struck,
Theodor Herzl,
etching.

several editions of the *Jüdischer Almanach*,[9] and it was used to adorn the official Congress postcard of 1909 in Hamburg and that of 1913, which was held in Herzl's city, Vienna (illus. 41). Numerous photographs of Zionist groups conspicuously include a reproduction of the Struck etching (illus. 70).[10] There is no evidence that Herzl, Struck, or the Zionist Organization tried to control the promulgation and hawking of likenesses of the work. In addition to postcards and pictures per se, David Tartakover has shown how Herzl's image, often a crude version of the Struck etching, decorated hundreds of consumer goods, such as teapots, drinking glasses, pocket watches and cigarette packets.[11] The sentimental attachment to the Struck etching of Herzl might also have been enhanced due to the respect accorded the artist Hermann Struck, a German–Jew who was a founder of the Orthodox arm of the Zionist movement, Mizrachi. Struck was known, as well, for sympathetically depicting East European Jews, the *Ostjuden*.[12] The affection for Struck the man seems to have abetted appreciation for Struck the artist.[13]

The next most popular, and likewise next most frequently appropriated, picture of Herzl was a view of him, photographed by E. M. Lilien, overlooking the Rhine Bridge in Basel during the First Zionist Congress (see illus. 5). Similar to Struck, Lilien was well known in Zionist circles, and considered to be a great 'national' artist. Although he was not traditionally observant, Zionists thought it notable that he hailed from the Galician ghetto.[14] Lilien was primarily identified,

41 Struck's etching (illus. 40) in an Art Nouveau setting. Postcard for the Eleventh Zionist Congress (Vienna, 1913).

42 E. M. Lilien's post-card for the Fifth Zionist Congress (London, 1900). The Hebrew inscription is a verse from the Amidah, a central prayer in Jewish liturgy: 'Let our eyes witness Your loving return to Zion.'

43 Herzl with a female 'Zion' carrying the flag. Drawing by S. Roukhomovsky printed on a postcard.

however, with a pen-and-ink drawing, an agricultural scene showing the regenerating Zion, that was used for the Fifth Zionist Congress postcard and Zionist fundraising appeals (illus. 42).[15] Lilien's earlier, impressive photographic effort identified Herzl with Basel, the European locale most associated with the movement and its Congress. For the next century, this picture would serve as a synecdoche for Zionism, encompassing the vast ideological and historical sweep of the movement. Herzl's glance in the picture suggested that, although he was above the Rhine, he was contemplating the Jewish future in a faraway place. Herzl himself was pleased with this picture. It easily melded with the epigraph of his utopian novel, *Altneuland* (Old-new Land), 'If you will it, it is not a dream.' The German of the original, 'Wenn ihr wollt ist es kein Maerchen' was supplanted in favour of a later Hebrew translation, which became the lyric of a folk song: 'Im tirtsu, eyn zo agadah.' One postcard using this motto showed it in Hebrew, German and French (illus. 43). I argued above that the Rhine

58

Bridge image might be used to illustrate the instability of supposedly realistic images, in that after Herzl's death this picture was imposed on a view of Jerusalem and other settings, which were used for Jewish National Fund stamps and other publicity.

Numerous artists, inspired by Herzl, turned their talents to trying to capture his spirit, such as Friedrich Baer (who sculpted Herzl immediately before his turn to Zionism), B. Marmorsten, Leopold Pilichowski, Jakob Loew, S. Kretschmer, Max Kurtzweil, Arpad Kopai, S. Roukomovsky, J. Rosintal (illus. 44; see also illus. 11, lower left), Alfred Nossig and Boris Schatz.[16] The majority of these are realistic, some clearly modelled on well-known photographs. Occasionally, though, Herzl would be placed in an anachronistic setting, such as the eighteenth century (illus. 45) or biblical times (see illus. 7). E. M. Lilien designed a stained-glass window for the Hamburg B'nai Brith, and illustrations for a Bible, depicting Herzl as Moses.[17] But the most popular picture proved to be the Struck etching, and the photographs – including the Rhine Bridge view, which was mounted on to other settings – were dearer than most drawings, paintings, or sculptures.

There are many resettings of a side-view photograph of Herzl, with arms folded; after 1904 the portrait or postcard version sometimes had

44 J. Rosintal, *Herzl Opening the Zionist Congress*. Postcard.

45 Max Kurtzweil, Painting showing Herzl in a romanticized period scene; there are several similar pictures.

46 One of the more popular Herzl portraits.

47 David Wolffsohn with a quote meant to underscore Jewish solidarity. Postcard.

a black border, to denote mourning (illus. 46).[18] Although this particular pose is distinctive, other frontal portraits of Herzl are reminiscent of photographs of Jewish sages, and even Jewish family-member portraits, often featuring the departed's thick beard.[19] Despite the fact that Herzl's beard was neatly trimmed, there was something believed to be Jewish and even messianic about it. Two of Herzl's closest associates in the movement, Max Nordau and David Wolffsohn, also boasted full complements of facial hair. Somehow the majestic and the rabbinical could be construed in the bushy beards; of Wolffsohn it was said that he looked the part of a leader: calm and manly.[20]

So as not to mistake the traditionally Jewish aspect of these images, picture-postcards of these bearded heroes were sometimes accompanied by quotations. One, of David Wolffsohn, quotes a Congress address of his intoning in Hebrew: 'One God, one people, one land, one language' (illus. 47). In truth, Wolffsohn began the speech in Hebrew, but he delivered most of it in the Congress vernacular, German. Likewise, a popular postcard and portrait image of Nordau was embellished with the following statement, attributed to him: 'We carry our Judaism like a jewel' (illus. 48). Interestingly, the quotation is in Yiddish, and it is not certain if Nordau actually knew more than a smattering of Yiddish. Furthermore, Nordau was famous for having

48 Max Nordau accompanied by a quote intended to make him appear supportive of a traditional variety of Judaism that he in fact rejected for himself. Postcard.

broken with traditional Judaism by scorning all forms of organized religion as part and parcel of civilization's 'conventional lies'. Herzl, especially after his death, was pictured amidst traditional, distressed-looking Jews, most of whom seem unaware that he is with them (illus. 49).

To be sure, the notion of authority, Jewishness and moral righteousness associated with a full beard was not confined to Zionism; it could be found in other secular-Jewish quarters. The Marxist–revisionist labour advocate Isaac Hourwich appeared in official portraits boasting a bushy, 'academic' beard, which was seen as aptly fitting his burly physique;[21] such pictures of Hourwich recalled as well a style of rabbinic portraiture. And it should come as no surprise that both Herzl and Jacob Gordin, a pillar of the Yiddish theatre, were noted for their 'Assyrian' beards (illus. 50). Descriptions of Gordin were virtually interchangeable with those of Herzl, as Gordin was esteemed as 'A handsome man, with dark flashing eyes [and a] black Assyrian beard [possessing a] proud bearing, and polished manners . . . He stood taller and straighter than those around him.' Both were seen as offering 'a perfect image' to youth.[22] 'The elegance that naturally belonged to Herzl' was ascribed, in similar terms, to Gordin.[23] 'His appearance', wrote the actress Bessie Thomashevsky, 'impressed all of us. He was tall and thin, with a remarkably handsome, noble face; deep, intelligent

49 Even after his death, Herzl was portrayed as a living presence among Jews in need. Postcard.

50 Jacob Gordin (1853–1909): Gordin styled himself as guiding the Jews towards higher culture.

eyes; a beautiful black beard, neatly trimmed; a great head of thick, black, curly hair, combed down to his nape . . .' The critic Shmuel Niger (brother of Baruch Charney Vladeck) recalled that Gordin's 'appearance was a part of his self. It was an expression of the strength he exerted, an emanation from his soul.'[24] In addition to such physical attributes, Gordin had also been a 'leader of a utopian Jewish agrarian movement before moving to New York in 1891'.[25] Perhaps it is not coincidental that both Herzl and Gordin were seen as arbiters of good taste. As vehicles for transforming Jewish hopes and dreams, there are a number of affinities that may be discerned between the leading lights of Zionism, Jewish labour, territorialism, the Yiddish theatre, and the founders of the Hollywood movie studios, as all of them aspired to influence and elevate what they saw as a debased Jewish culture. The

62

51 This group portrait of the 'Democratic Faction' includes Weizmann and Martin Buber (1878–1965) (in the same row but one person away from Herzl); Lilien is at the bottom right; next to him is Motzkin, one of the movement's more formidable intellectuals. Despite this group's reputed opposition to Herzl, all of its members posed with him.

52 Not the first Zionist postcard to feature an American flag.

Hollywood moguls, however, did not become icons in the same way, as they worked behind the scenes to fashion an idealized social order that would be embraced by everyone – not simply Jews – in the United States. They sought vehemently to distance themselves from allegations that they were advancing particular Jewish interests in their film production.[26]

Herzl's presence at the Zionist Congresses gave his faithful the chance to be photographed with him. There are numerous pictures of him with his fellow journalists, national contingents and diverse Zionist subgroups and individual delegates. Even the clique that saw itself as his first intra-Zionist 'opposition', the 'Democratic Faction', insisted on having its photo taken with the leader (illus. 51).[27] This seemed to indicate both an urge to identify with Herzl, and to show that he too was one of his people. Photographs of Herzl were not simply icons; hundreds of Zionists could boast of being in the same picture as their leader. Often these groups' portraits were reproduced as postcards as well. Likewise, after Herzl's death, Max Nordau, David Wolffsohn, Nahum Sokolow and Chaim Weizmann assumed pride of place in the centre of group portraits. Both Nordau and Wolffsohn can be seen among delegates from the United States at the Eighth Zionist Congress (The Hague, 1907), in a postcard published by the 'New York Bargain Store' of Greensburg, Pennsylvania (illus. 52). All of these Zionist leaders existed both as icons and among the people.

Herzl and Nordau frequently were shown together in the same media (illus. 53). It was important that they were perceived as friends, as Zionism, like other liberal national movements, maintained male friendship in high regard as a cornerstone of nationhood.[28] Jewish socialists, too, experienced their brotherhood as one of the heady aspects of their politics.[29] In addition to Nordau's status as a celebrity-intellectual, it was thought that his presence testified to the good sense of Herzl's idea of a Jewish state, which was derided by Zionism's critics as a symptom of a mental breakdown or megalomania. Herzl's portrait also appeared in postcards with other Zionist leaders – including those with whom he feuded. Interestingly, one can find personalities such as Nathan Birnbaum, Israel Zangwill and Bernard Lazare in Zionist publicity long after their public denunciations of the movement (illus. 54, 55, 56). All three had a major falling-out with either Herzl or Zionism, yet their images were promulgated nonetheless. On the most transparent level, showing them with Herzl was understandable, as they had all been prominent in the launch of Zionism. But there seems to have been careful thought given to the casting of these personalities.

Nathan Birnbaum was especially popular among the Austrian students who provided an important base for Zionism's growth and day-to-day operations.[30] After Herzl's ascendancy, though, Birnbaum turned to Yiddishism (as a foil to Hebraism) and eventually to anti-Zionist Orthodoxy as a means to find his own way to an authentic Jewishness. He became the premier icon of a mass Jewish movement intended to counter Zionism – Agudas Yisroel – and Birnbaum would long continue to inspire the anti-Zionist Haredim (ultra-Orthodox) worldwide.[31] Zangwill was one of the more recognized British supporters of Zionism, and a popular Jewish writer of the fin-de-siècle, but he, like Birnbaum, diverted himself to an alternate course. In Zangwill's case, the turn was to non-Palestinian territorialism. Nevertheless, two pictures of Herzl, Zangwill and Herzl's mother were among Zionist favourites (illus. 57, 58). In order to illustrate the Zionist connection to Britain, Herzl sometimes was pictured with Rabbi Moses Gaster, the 'Haham', or Sephardic chief rabbi of Britain (see illus. 55). Gaster was in fact an important ally, who had provided Herzl's entrée at mass meetings in London's East End.[32] Even Gaster, though, had something of a chequered relationship with Herzl, as in

54 Herzl and fellow Zionists, including Leo Pinsker (1821–1891) (bottom right), whom he never met.

55 Herzl and his esteemed cohort: Bernard Lazare (1865–1903), Max Mandelstamm (1839–1912), Nordau and Gaster. Postcard.

the early years of the movement he was accused of acting as 'a rival of and competitor to Herzl rather than his out-and-out supporter'.[33] Bernard Lazare, too, had momentarily been a Zionist star, when he was praised during the Second Zionist Congress for his prescience and courage in bringing the Dreyfus Affair to light.[34] But the radical-socialist dimension of Zionism was not pronounced enough for Lazare.[35] Showing him alongside Herzl indicated that there was a Zionist following of significance in France – which was not the case until late in the interwar years. In France, support for the Alliance Israélite Universelle tapped into the philanthropic wellsprings from which Zionism typically grew, so the movement's taking hold in

56 Herzl and colleagues: Nathan Birnbaum (1864–1937), who became an ardent anti-Zionist; Israel Zangwill, who abandoned Zionism for 'territorialist' solutions beyond Palestine; and Sokolow.

France was especially problematic. Despite the tensions between Herzl and these men, they continued to be assembled into collages as Zionism's founding fathers.

Perhaps the most effective joining of Herzl with an adversary is the much-reproduced composite portrait purporting to be of the 'delegates' to the First Zionist Congress (illus. 59). It does not represent all of the delegates, as the number was greater, but it distorts the actual Congress in other respects as well. It would come to grace meeting rooms, reading rooms, Jewish offices and schools and synagogue rooms. Of course Herzl is largest and in the centre, and Nordau is next to him. Located in the row below – giving the appearance that he was among the delegates – is Ahad Ha-Am, who was indeed there but as a journalist and curiosity-seeker. Herzl personally offered him the opportunity to attend as a delegate, and even to address the Congress in Hebrew, if he wished.[36] He did not; nor is there any record that Ahad Ha-Am even acknowledged Herzl's letter. Ahad Ha-Am publicly admonished the gathering for being shrill and aping the Gentiles. An exceptional moment for him, however, was Nordau's keynote address, which he found exhilarating.[37] Still, the Congress group-portrait gives the impression not only of Ahad Ha-Am's presence at the meeting, but implies that he participated in a more involved and constructive manner. Nahum Sokolow, too, is pictured as a delegate. Although he entered the Congress a sceptical journalist, he claimed to have left it a

57 Herzl among delegates to the tempestuous Sixth Zionist Congress (Basel, 1903),
which debated whether or not to investigate
the British offer of East Africa (the 'Uganda
Plan').

58 Israel Zangwill (1864–1926) with Herzl
and Herzl's mother, Jeanette: Many of
Herzl's family pictures became Zionist
pictures.

fervent Zionist. Sokolow became a second-tier Zionist icon, famous
for his moderating influence at the helm of the movement in the wake
of the tempestuous rule of Chaim Weizmann. This Congress portrait,
along with the Herzl Rhine Bridge photograph, seemed to encapsulate
the Zionists' shining moment of their entrance on to the world stage, in
the Basel Congress of 1897.

A desire to annex the pre-Herzlian history of the movement for
Palestine settlement since 1881, Hibbat and Hovevei Zion, also motivated the construction of Zionist images. A number of postcards and
portraits of Herzl, or Herzl with Nordau, were shown with Dr Max
Mandelstamm, 'a distinguished ophthalmologist from Kiev' and a
founder of Hibbat Zion in Russia (illus. 60).[38] True to the image,

59 This ostensibly authoritative picture of delegates to the First Zionist Congress in fact includes some individuals who were not delegates and omits others.

David Vital writes that Mandelstamm played a role 'of genuine substance' in the movement both before and after Herzl's rise.[39] In addition to Birnbaum, the portrait of Hermann Schapira in the orbit of Herzl also was meant to show the continuity between Herzl and those who had blazed the trail, particularly in Jewish university-student nationalism, before his rise. Schapira, a professor of mathematics, was probably the second-oldest delegate to the Congress, and had recruited a group of his Heidelberg University students to accompany him to Basel (illus. 61).

Herzl and Nordau also were pictured with other Jewish and world leaders, which speaks volumes about the aspirations, if not pretensions of the movement. A privately produced greeting card, apparently made for members of an early Zionist society, situated Herzl and

60 An elaborate, privately produced greetings card featuring Max Mandelstamm as a leading Zionist.

61 Hermann Schapira (1810–1898): The mathematics professor from Heidelberg who accompanied a group of Jewish-nationalist students to the First Zionist Congress. Schapira is credited with originating the idea of the Jewish National Fund.

62 Reverse of the elaborate greetings card (illus. 60), which makes Christopher Columbus and George Washington into proto-Zionists.

Nordau – as well as Moses Gaster, Bernard Lazare and Max Mandelstamm – alongside Christopher Columbus and George Washington (illus. 62). Herzl was, indeed, accustomed to being introduced as the new Moses or Columbus, which he dismissed as exaggerations, yet he made no effort to dispel such rhetoric.[40] In a less ostentatious manner, this trend was continued, as Chaim Weizmann was similarly depicted on the same page with United States' President Warren Harding, British Prime Ministers David Lloyd George and Ramsay MacDonald, Lord Balfour and General Allenby during the Mandatory years (illus. 63, 64). The Zionists therefore legitimated

63 Weizmann surrounded by political heavyweights, including the American President Warren Harding. From *Palaestina-Bilder-Korrespondenz* (May 1929).

themselves through their association with non-Jewish world leaders and luminaries.

Zionists were not alone in adopting this visual strategy. Showing Weizmann with British leaders was similar to the depiction of US Jewish socialists (and communists) with the non-Jewish Eugene Debs (illus. 65; see also illus. 22, top left) or claiming Norman Thomas as a fully fledged member of the Arbeter Ring.[41] The United Hebrew Trades, in their jubilee book, gave pride of place to the greetings by New York (Jewish) Governor Herbert Lehman;[42] and Jewish communists boasted John Reed as a comrade-in-arms.[43] Integrating non-Jews in this manner was a way of showing that the Jewish movements were full and equal partners with like-minded Gentiles. Although these pictures were not intended to be duplicitous, they might have given the impression that the non-Jews were more engaged with Jewish concerns than they actually were. For instance, the appropriation of Eleanor Roosevelt correctly reflected the fact that she was passionately devoted to US and world Jewry. The picturing of her husband, Franklin Delano Roosevelt, on the other hand, suggested a more tenuous proposition, that caring about Jews was one of his greatest priorities (illus. 66). The embrace of Franklin Roosevelt, though, was

64 Weizmann with a different set of leaders. From *Palaestina-Bilder-Korrespondenz* (October 1928).

65 Obituary for Eugene Debs in the Jewish Communist paper *Der Hamer*, December 1926.

an accurate if painful rendering of American Jewry's intense affection for the president. Furthermore, although modern Jewish historiography has understandably focused on Franklin Roosevelt's role in the Holocaust, there has been considerably less attention paid to the fact that he was overwhelmingly sympathetic to Jewry in organized labour.[44]

Still, Jewish icons on their own were more critical than were non-Jews claimed for Jewish causes. For Zionists at the fin-de-siècle, the quantity and variety of portraits and postcards of Nordau is surpassed only by the amount for Herzl; Nordau provided, in some respects, the perfect complement to Herzl. Like Herzl, he was a journalist and *litterateur*, writing primarily in German. His authority as a physician and scientist enhanced his position as a best-selling author; he was a featured journalist for newspapers from Budapest, Berlin, Frankfurt and Vienna. Although he tended to avoid Jewish topics in his novels and social criticism before 1897, Nordau's traditional Jewish background as the son of a modest rabbi constituted part of the mythology of his public image.[45] Surely, though, his star was beginning to fall precipitously as his cultural arch-conservatism and anti-Freudian psychology became more outmoded. One of the most unusual efforts to see Nordau as a great Jew is a postcard portrait done in micrograph,

66 Franklin Roosevelt endorsing a Zionist bond drive. From *Kinder-Tshurnal* (April 1943).

a tiny Hebrew translation of the introduction of his best-selling book, *Conventional Lies of Our Civilization* (illus. 67). Even before he appeared at the First Congress, many Jews identified Nordau as a representative of Jewish concerns, and as an exemplar of positive Jewish characteristics.[46] His looks gave rise to comparisons with the ancient sages or prophets; his iconoclasm led several devotees to see him as a modern Jeremiah.[47] Some of the portraits and postcard pictures were drawn or painted by Nordau's daughter, Maxa.[48] E. M. Lilien produced a drawing of Nordau, but it did not circulate as widely as the half-dozen most common photographs.[49] A sepia portrait of Nordau, the frontispiece of his *Zionistische Schriften* (illus. 68), was the most popular of the Nordau images, which was also used as the setting for the above-mentioned Yiddish quote.

In its initial stage, before the First World War, Zionism promoted Herzl and Nordau as great Jewish leaders, concomitant with the claim that the first flowering of 'a modern natural' Jewry was underway in Palestine; it was seen as 'a focal point of immeasurable moral value for the entire Diaspora'.[50] Certainly the hundreds of images proclaiming and illustrating the new Jewish life in Palestine, emphasizing the agricultural basis of the society in which Jews were excelling as workers and farmers, had an impact on the ways Jews saw themselves – or at least the potential for themselves or other Jews.[51] In this regard, images of Zionists such as David Ben-Gurion and Berl Katznelson were more significant as types – New Zionist Jews – than as individuals.[52]

But Zionists and non-Zionists did not necessarily have to look to Palestine to find examples of physically emboldened Jews who asserted their Jewishness with pride. This role was taken up, with aplomb, by nationalized student societies and so-called Jewish gymnasts (illus. 69). The university-based student groups were famous for attempting to prove their mettle through fighting duels with non-Jewish fraternity members. Many pictures showed their sabres (illus. 70), as well as the

Dr Max NORDAU

67 This micrograph, a strange
tribute to Nordau, was obviously
a painstaking effort. The picture
is made of a Hebrew translation
of the introduction to Nordau's
book *Conventional Lies of Our
Civilization*. Postcard.

68 Nordau's portrait was sold
separately, and several versions
appeared on postcards.

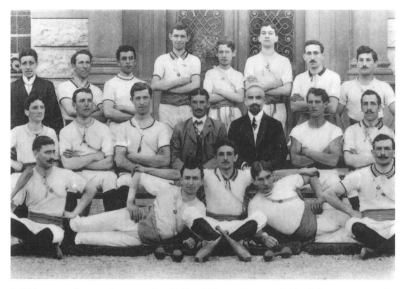

69 This group of gymnasts appeared at the Tenth Zionist Congress in Basel; there were several such demonstrations during the Congress days.

manly trappings of beer and cigarettes (illus. 71); they proudly displayed their ribbons, medals, sashes and caps, emblazoned with the Shield of David (illus. 72). Complementing his reputation as expert fencer, as well as a horseman, Nordau was famous for spreading the message that gymnastics would help instil 'calm confidence in his own strength' for the New Jew. A muscular Jewry would help win Jewish honour; respect and pride in one's Jewishness became a matter of public display through athletics.[53] The scholar of Jewish mysticism Gershom Scholem recalled that his uncle Theobald held Zionism as 'a kind of spiritual liberation that manifested itself in a somewhat paradoxical way. He was one of the founders of the Jewish gymnastics association Bar Kochba and performed for Theodor Herzl at the Basel Zionist Congress of 1903. A photo of the squad of gymnasts with Herzl in the middle hung in the parlour of his home.'[54]

The Jewish gymnasts, members of organized Jewish youth movements, and university student societies implicitly conveyed the notion in their self-representations that Europe and the United States could serve as a training ground for a new type of 'tough' Jew.[55] Thus Zionism helped open up a cultural space for the idealization of Jewish sports heroes. Muscular Jews, especially boxers, became important cultural icons in the United States, Britain, Germany and the Netherlands. The dissemination of their pictures, especially in the press, coincided with the growth of radio and movie audiences for

71 A manly individual with a beer, larger than the stereotypical small glass supposedly preferred by Jewish fraternity men. From 'Barissia'.

72 Jewish national student. From 'Barissia'.

prizefights. Numerous articles appeared in the Jewish and Zionist press praising the role played by the eighteenth-century boxer, Daniel Mendoza, for helping make possible toleration of the Jews in Britain, as well as for developing boxing as a 'scientific' sport. Among the more notable twentieth-century pugilists were Benny Leonard, who retired in 1925 as undefeated lightweight champion, and Barney Ross (born Barnet David Rosofsky) from the United States.

73 Ted 'Kid' Lewis (born Gerson Mendeloff, 1894–1970): One of Britain's notable Jewish fighters, Lewis was revered for his dignity and modesty.

Traditional Jewish origins and 'practice' was central to the image that Barney Ross and others cultivated. The story related by singer Eddie Cantor, in his introduction to Ross's autobiography, is typical: 'I remember walking in on him in a little alcove just off the training ring with its smell of linament and human sweat, and finding him hunched over various books of the Prophets and other parts of the Bible. This was the literature he always took to training camps – not comic books, Westerns, or detective stories.'[56] In Britain Ted 'Kid' Lewis (illus. 73)[57] and Jack 'Kid' Berg were among the big Jewish fighters of their time,[58]

74 Ben Bril, the Dutch champion of 1939, proudly displaying his Magen David.

as was Ben Bril, the Dutch champion of 1939 (illus. 74). Both Berg and Lewis gained a significant American following, which boosted their fortunes in Britain.[59] Although these boxers were not necessarily Zionist, many were unmistakably identified as ethnic-national Jews, often clothing themselves in blue and white and a Magen David. In boxing lore, 'an old time fighter called Harry Stone' originated the ritual of wearing a *talit* and *tefillin* into the ring before a fight, which was imitated by Kid Berg.[60] Even some non-Jews, notably the fighter Max Baer, claimed Jewish origins as a means to attract a Jewish follow-

75 An official portrait of Chaim Weizmann.

ing, and because Jewish fighters were thought to be savvy in the ring. Not surprisingly, during the years of Nazi control, the *Jüdische Rundschau* – the leading Central European Zionist organ – devoted ever-increasing space to the exploits of Jewish athletes, especially boxers. As most news was heavily censored, reports of Maccabiah events and intra-Jewish competitions came to constitute a substantial share of the paper.

The comprehensive transformation of the Jewish people, according to Zionist ideology, could take place only in Palestine. Nevertheless, the movement's heads, in the years between the wars, cultivated the legends of diaspora Jews, and a few non-Jews, as Zionist heroes. In the next decades Chaim Weizmann, Henrietta Szold, Louis Brandeis and

Albert Einstein were especially venerated. Their portrayal by the movement served not only to highlight their status and achievements but also to create an impression that a broad consensus existed about the correctness and likelihood of success of the Zionist project. Each of them represented traits with which the movement wished to identify, and their public endorsement gave Zionism lustre. A common thread that unites the projection of these figures, and complemented other efforts to nationalize Western Jewry, was the claim that they exemplified Zionism's affinity to a secular, humanistic culture.

The evolving mythology of the movement underscored that it was primarily the efforts of Chaim Weizmann that paved the way for the Balfour Declaration. The Balfour Declaration was one of the few shining moments for organized Jewry in the midst of the First World War, which was disastrous for Eastern Jewry and seriously called into question Jewish integration in Britain and Germany. Zionist pamphlets boasted that 'no statesman in the history of the world' had accomplished what Weizmann had 'without a state, without an army, and without the requisite financial means'.[61] He was 'the living symbol of the Jewish Palestine-movement of our generation': not only 'a leader', but 'the Leader'.[62] Certainly in form, Weizmann's official portrait bears a striking resemblance to that of Lenin (illus. 75). Weizmann was the first Zionist politician after Herzl to be widely perceived as a respectable agent for the movement in the corridors of power.[63]

Along with the acclaim of his brilliant statecraft, Weizmann was

79

77 The serious, studious, judicious Louis Brandeis.

touted as a first-rate scientist. His identity as a 'great chemist' was seen as interwoven with his role as 'a great statesman'.[64] In the Zionist press and pamphlet literature, Weizmann's brain-power was a favourite topic.[65] Perhaps the pictures of Weizmann's shining bald pate were a way of suggesting the powerful mind within (illus. 76). After training at the technological university at Charlottenburg, he pursued a career in research in Britain, eventually assuming a position (but not a professorship, as is often said) at Manchester University.[66] His work was significant to the British war effort in developing a better acetone for explosives. Through the comments of those speaking about him, and also by sprinkling his own speeches and writings with references to science or chemistry in particular, Weizmann sought to demonstrate that the Jews' return to Palestine was consistent with a 'scientific' world-view, not simply a messianic-romantic illusion. His own understanding of scientific principles, he extrapolated, translated into the ability to lead the movement in a most propitious direction.[67]

Despite his prominence as a scientist, no other Zionist figure simultaneously bridged the worlds of modern civilization and a romanticized view of 'authentic' Eastern Jewry as did Weizmann.[68] He made the most of his *yiddishkayt* origins. He was a child of the ghetto who had struggled to make his way in the secular world, in academic and applied science and politics, and he seemed to have mastered them all. After his rise in Zionist ranks, there was little recognition that Weizmann had envisioned Zionism as a rejection and transcendence of the ghetto, as is clear from his personal correspondence.[69] Nevertheless, the view of Weizmann as an *Ostjude par excellence* was trotted out numerous times during Weizmann's feud with Louis Brandeis and the so-called Brandeis group, as he was extolled as the leader most in touch with the true 'folk soul' of the Jewish people.[70]

Irma Lindheim, a president of Hadassah, offers a keen insight into why the fierce opposition to Weizmann was not more effective in having him removed. 'I understand why the word "seductive" is often used in describing him', Lindheim observed. 'His words, his meanings, are sharp, penetrating, incisive, but he speaks in a voice so melodious and low, so pleasing to the senses, that instead of arousing resistance which his militant words would ordinarily evoke, his voice insinuates itself into the consciousness of the listener.'[71] Thousands upon thousands of Jews saw and heard him directly, as Weizmann was a tireless campaigner for Zionism; his itinerary was loaded with stops in small towns as well as metropolitan centres.

If Weizmann filled the role of the dyed-in-the-wool Eastern Jew, showing the compatibility of Zionism and *yiddishkayt*, whose reputation could stand independent of his Zionist attachment, Louis D. Brandeis accomplished this with regard to the United States (illus. 77). He personified the compatibility of Zionism and Americanism.[72] He was a 'true-blue' American, whose credentials as a leading light of United States legal theory and progressive social thought were impeccable; furthermore, Brandeis was widely seen as sympathetic to improving the plight of the working-class Jewish masses.[73] Those such as Isaac Hourwich, who believed that Brandeis was compliant to the demands of management above labour, constituted a dogged but small minority among Jews. Brandeis endowed the Zionist movement with a sparkling intellectual grandeur, and demonstrated that Zionism was in harmony with the best minds and interests of the United States. In particular, Zionist youth were thrilled by his appearance on the scene. As 'a knight errant' battling the 'social order of vested interests', he aroused a cult of 'hero-worship'. Brandeis was said to embody 'a sense of justice and a moral quality that set him apart as the highest type of the Lincolnian liberal fighting for the rights of the common people'.[74]

The path leading Louis D. Brandeis to a passionate interest in

Jewish politics became part of Jewish and Zionist lore. He had moved from an abject secularism to a burning interest in the Jewish question. The prevailing theme of thumbnail sketches was that he, like Herzl, Nordau, Zangwill and a few other key leaders – reaching back to the biblical Moses – had 'found his way back' to Judaism and the Jews. His life could easily be interpreted according to the Zionist theme of exile, return and redemption; most often, he was favourably likened to Herzl.[75] After his address concerning the Arab riots of 1930, the 'Zionist page' of *Der Tog*, the New York Yiddish daily, reported that

It was as a speech and reminder by a great patriot and statesman. Justly it can be said that the epoch of the bloody events in Palestine may be divided into two periods: Before the speech by Brandeis and after the speech. At the moment when the speech reached the Jews world over, a spiritual transfiguration took place within us. We have heard once again the call of Herzl, and anew in our ears resounded the voice of World Zionism.[76]

Inside and outside Zionist circles Brandeis frequently was credited with having 'a characteristically Hebrew spirit'[77] or 'an intensely Jewish soul'; his role as a maker and moulder of law was seen as endemic to Jewry, a mark of the Jewish propensity for legal study engaging its sharpest minds. It was said to be no coincidence that, in an earlier time of crisis, the people of Israel were led by 'Judges' and, during the trauma of the Great War, Louis Brandeis stepped forward to lead.[78] One writer's description of Brandeis as combining the characteristics of Moses with those of Abraham Lincoln was typical of the Jewish-American synthesis that the justice seemed to represent.[79] Although Brandeis had no beard, it was not difficult to associate him with rabbinical and talmudic authority, as he was often pictured in his judicial robe.

In no other national setting had the fate of the Zionist Organization rested on the shoulders of one individual as Zionism in the United States depended on Brandeis.[80] It proved to be a tremendous setback for the movement when, from 1921 to 1931, Brandeis was clearly in conflict with Weizmann, the leader of the World Zionist Organization, and Louis Lipsky, the president of the American Zionist Federation. In the years that Brandeis was a member of the opposition, the popularity of Zionism in the United States suffered a sharp decline.[81]

Among Brandeis's close associates in the movement were Jacob De Haas, Julian Mack, Robert Szold, Felix Frankfurter and Rabbi Stephen S. Wise. Wise, like Brandeis, was a leading spokesman and advocate for a wide range of progressive politics, and personified a bridge between Reform Judaism, American officialdom and the

Zionist Organization. A newspaper photo of Wise standing between Albert Einstein and David Dubinsky, smiling broadly and shaking hands, encapsulates his role as well as any single image (illus. 78). He was the most visible, besides Brandeis himself, among the members of the 'Brandeis group'. Wise had been an early adherent of Zionism, and in 1898 attended the Second Zionist Congress in Basel; he recalled seeing Herzl as an 'ancient monarch of the Near East . . . At once, I felt a bond with him, apart from my unreserved acceptance of his leadership.'[82] In 1922 Wise established the Jewish Institute of Religion, which held unequivocal Jewish solidarity as its primary objective, as earlier with Brandeis he had helped to found the American Jewish Congress, with its goal of 'uniting within a democratic framework all Jewish groups for common action on Jewish affairs' (1916). This idea was expanded into the World Jewish Congress, which materialized in 1936.[83] Wise was effective as an institution-builder, and he served to represent these wide-ranging bodies; but he was no sycophant to the Zionist, Jewish or US government establishments.

The argument has been made that Stephen S. Wise, 'the foremost American Jewish leader of the 1930s and 1940s',[84] misread the unfolding catastrophe in Europe and the Nazi menace, and might have attempted other or more valiant efforts to save – or even inform – his

79 Wise making it clear that he is a
force to be reckoned with.

80 Wise the tough rabbi.

81 Henrietta Szold with other leaders who resigned from the Zionist Executive in Palestine in 1930. Drawing by Erna Grossman (?), from *Palaestina-Bilder-Korrespondenz* (February 1930).

endangered co-religionists. The standard evaluation of Wise is that 'his total trust in Roosevelt was not an asset to American or European Jews'.[85] This assessment does not reflect the courageous stances for which he was recognized during his time. As opposed to being viewed primarily in light of Jewish foreign affairs, Wise was seen in the context of the appeal for Jewish workers' rights. In response to 'the first great strike of women in American history', the waistcoat makers in 1909, Wise praised the strikers and asserted that 'the synagogue', too, was compelled to stand behind the workers.[86] Stephen S. Wise's official portraits, accentuating his firm jaw and piercing gaze, suggest a personality respected as resolute, if not tenacious (illus. 79, 80).

Both Brandeis and Wise distinguished themselves as fighters for the rights of Jewish women, and sought to allow them greater responsibilities in politics generally, as well as in Zionism. One of Brandeis's roles, in this regard, was to be the founding patron of Hadassah, the Women's Zionist Organization of America. As much as Brandeis was the most important force behind the Hadassah organization, there is no equal to Henrietta Szold, in any aspect of Zionism, who so successfully established a part of the movement in his or her own image (illus. 81).[87] Born into a prominent rabbinical family in Baltimore, Szold developed a consuming passion for Zionism, and during the years of the First World War she devoted tremendous energy to organizing the

THE PALESTINE PHOTO SERVICE

ALBERT EINSTEIN,
DER SCHÖPFER DER RELATIVITÄTSTHEORIE,
DER GROSSE JUDE,
FEIERTE AM 14. MÄRZ SEINEN FÜNFZIGSTEN GEBURTSTAG

American Zionist Medical Unit, which was the seed of Hadassah. In less than a decade Hadassah was one of the most formidable parts of world Zionism, a feat which is even more striking if one considers the dearth of women's participation earlier in the movement's history. From any perspective, Szold's accomplishment was astounding.[88] But the accolades she received rarely did justice to the obstacles she was forced to overcome from within the Zionist establishment.

Henrietta Szold was utilized as a symbol of Zionism as one of the world's first political movements 'to base its constitution [sic] upon the principle of absolute equality for all adherents irrespective of sex', in which any position could be held by a woman.[89] Whereas throughout the West women seemed to be striving for equality, Szold showed that in Zionism it had been achieved. But the idolization of Henrietta Szold was not exclusive to any single Zionist contention or agenda; she was seen as a pioneering humanist more than as a feminist. For instance, under her tutelage, Hadassah became famous for not discriminating between Jews and non-Jews. Szold, like the philosopher Martin Buber, gained a reputation for advocating open dialogue and an empathetic

83 This portrait of Einstein, which circulated among Zionists, was dedicated to Arthur Ruppin (1923).

understanding of Palestine's Arabs. Certainly this strain of Zionist discourse helped facilitate the efforts of non-Zionist bodies, such as the Gewerkschaften (United Hebrew Trades), to lend support to Zionism. Such groups were adamant that their backing of Zionism should not in any way compromise the greater workers' struggle in Palestine which included Arabs as well as Jews. They took the Histadruth at its word

84 Einstein with Stephen Wise, who, like Nahum Goldmann, counted his friendship with Einstein as one of the joys of his life.

that it was actively seeking equality and brotherhood between Jews and Arabs.[90] The complex history that already had eroded this possibility rarely surfaced, however, in either organization's polemics. And at a time when Zionism in the United States was foundering, Hadassah was its strongest and most resilient component. Nevertheless, in the Zionist realm the originality of Henrietta Szold was rarely as celebrated as her organizational skills. Little wonder that Szold is not to be found in the standard works as a significant Zionist 'thinker'.[91]

Above all, the figure treasured as diaspora Zionism's greatest claim to fame, who played an immeasurable role in the Jewish self-imagination, was Albert Einstein (illus. 82).[92] Zionists the world over wholeheartedly agreed that Professor Einstein was their most spectacular attraction. Strangely, he has not been given his due in most Zionist historiography. Einstein's importance in boosting Jewish pride in, and confidence in the general direction of, Zionism, and Jewish self-assertion in general, defies comparison. Few Zionists would have disputed that Einstein was

the personification of every great quality a man can have: goodness of heart, honesty, and boundless love for all living creatures. It would have been almost impossible to discover a character defect in him. But perhaps his most amaz-

88

ing quality was his absolute simplicity. He was what he was in a perfectly natural way, without any effort.[93]

Despite the fact that his theories were incomprehensible except to a very narrow elite, it was generally known that he 'introduced a new scientific conception of space and time and of their relation to the physical world'. It was likewise known, particularly among Jews, that 'the foremost Jewish genius of our age is a modest, unassuming, kindly gentleman, almost childlike in his simplicity, with a keen sense of humor'.[94]

Einstein's portrait became a universal symbol of scientific genius with a human face, and Zionists were ecstatic to be able to appropriate him as one of their own (illus. 83).[95] They showed his picture and talked about him on every possible occasion.[96] Everyone wanted to soak up his wisdom, meet him, shake his hand, and be photographed with him (illus. 84). His presence at public Zionist functions resulted in huge crowds that could barely control their adulation.[97] Whatever he had to say was taken as a solemn pronouncement to be pondered, regardless of its novelty.[98] Zionists also liked to believe that, when Einstein spoke, the rest of the world listened intently.[99] Whenever he took to the road his movements were tracked by Zionist organs with the fervour of gossip sheets looking for any scrap of information about a Hollywood celebrity;[100] his pilgrimages to Palestine were regarded as sacred events.[101]

Stories about Einstein, some of them apocryphal, became part of Zionist and Jewish lore. The best known (true) story is from the State of Israel: in 1952, upon the death of Chaim Weizmann, Einstein was offered the presidency of the State of Israel, albeit a largely ceremonial position – despite the fact that he did not live, and had never lived, in the country.[102] His brief response to the extraordinary request was perfectly in character:

I am deeply moved by the offer from our State of Israel, and at once saddened and ashamed that I cannot accept it. All my life I have dealt with objective matters, hence I lack both the natural aptitude and the experience to deal properly with people and to exercise official functions. For these reasons alone I should be unsuited to fulfill the duties of that high office, even if advancing age was not making increasing inroads on my strength. I am the more distressed over these circumstances because my relationship to the Jewish people has become my strongest human bond, ever since I became fully aware of our precarious situation in the world.[103]

Similar to the perception of Brandeis, Einstein, too, was seen as having a rather weak connection to Jewish culture and politics before

85 Jacob Israel De Haan, an ultra-orthodox Jew who attempted to gain favour with Arab governments.

his turn to Zionism.[104] Like Gershom Scholem, his encounter with East European Jews was pivotal in his attraction to Judaism and Zionism. Despite his sincere intolerance for chauvinism, Einstein was explicit about the necessity of a national movement for world Jewry, and Zionism in particular:

Before we can effectively combat anti-Semitism, we must first of all educate ourselves out of our slave-mentality which it betokens. We must have more dignity, more independence in our own ranks. Only when we have the courage to regard ourselves as a nation, when we respect ourselves, can we win the respect of others; or rather, the respect of others will then come of itself.

Einstein clearly articulated the notion that to be a Jew, and to be a Zionist, required an unconditional love for the entirety of the Jewish people, and especially the Jews' 'poor (East European) Jewish brethren', the *Ostjuden*.[105] 'Let us just leave anti-Semitism to the non-Jews', he wrote, 'and keep our hearts warm for our kith and kin.'[106] Not since Herzl's early addresses and writings had a Zionist leader's call for Jewish unity been received as a sign of integrity, generosity and compassion, as opposed to a tactical ploy. Also like Brandeis and Herzl, Einstein embodied the notion of 'returning to the fold'.[107] Again echoing the thought of Herzl, Einstein stated that 'I regard the growth of Jewish self-assertion as being in the interests of non-Jews as well as of

Jews. That was the main motive of my joining the Zionist ranks.'[108]

Yet Einstein went further than any other Zionist leader in defining and condoning the existence of Zionism in the diaspora, which made him uniquely suited for heroic stature in the Western Jewish communities, especially the United States. His was the most lucid argument articulated in support of diaspora-nationalism, without intoning the pious Zionist hope that all Jewry would eventually settle in Palestine. 'For me', Einstein wrote,

Zionism is not merely a question of colonization. The Jewish nation is a living thing, and the sentiment of Jewish nationalism must be developed both in Palestine and everywhere else. To deny the Jews' nationality in the Diaspora is, indeed, deplorable. If one adopts the point of view confining Jewish ethnic nationalism to Palestine, then to all intents and purposes one denies the existence of a Jewish people. In that case we should have the courage to carry through assimilation as quickly and as completely as possible.[109]

Although he freely admitted his disdain for 'undignified assimilationist cravings and strivings', Einstein nevertheless repeated Herzl's and Brandeis's claim that Zionism and other nationalities need not be mutually exclusive. There is no reason why the Zionist 'who remains true to his origin' should not 'also remain loyal to the State of which he is a subject. He who is faithless to one will also be faithless to the other.'[110]

In terms of his efforts for conciliation with Palestine's Arabs, Einstein was on the margins of Zionist politics. Rather than challenging him, however, there was usually no comment when he advocated the idea of a binational, Jewish-Arab state.[111] 'For him the domination of Jew over Arab in Palestine, or the perpetuation of hostilities between the two peoples, would mean the end of Zionism.'[112] Einstein was, therefore, a Zionist and national Jew whose appeal to the Jewish world at large was perhaps greater than any other in the twentieth century. The way Einstein was received suggests a blurring of conventional categories of esteem for integrity, super-intelligence, dignity, depth of spirit and even beauty. The magnetism of his image shows little sign of abating, although some seventy years after his pronouncements for Zionism his role in Jewish politics, and Zionism in particular, commands little notice. With the greatest amount of enthusiasm and conviction, Einstein was cited as exemplary of Zionism's claim to be inextricably connected with the greatest fruits of human civilization, and committed to the Jewish nation's development as a 'light unto the nations'.

On a more parochial level, Einstein was prized among Zionists for attracting converts to the cause, and for the apparent ease with which he was able to solicit donations, especially for the Hebrew University. He happened to join the movement at the precise moment when Chaim Weizmann created the Keren Hayesod (Palestine Foundation Fund), which reconfigured Zionism primarily as a fundraising movement oriented to the United States.

In no small part due to its overwhelming emphasis on fundraising after 1921, the movement developed the creed that support for Zionism was tantamount to support for Jewry and, concomitantly, that refusal to support mainstream Zionism was somehow anti-Jewish. It therefore became a kind of litmus test for Jewish loyalty, a stand that often intrudes on the evaluations of personalities in the *Encyclopaedia Judaica* – which was, after all, a Zionist creation. Within Zionism, though, the figure who emerged as the *enfant terrible* was Vladimir Jabotinsky. Although Jabotinsky had strong support in Palestine, his following in the West, at least before the Second World War, was minuscule. This is not to deny his intellectual power and charisma, but to recognize that his vision of Zionism was not among the more 'palatable' alternatives even to the movement's rank and file in the West.[113] It was only in South Africa, and to a lesser extent Ireland, that he seemed to be very influential among immigrant Jews.[114] After his death in 1940, and particularly after the rise to power of his professed disciple, Menahem Begin, Jabotinsky's star would rise to heights never attained during his lifetime. Before the war, however, in the West he was marginal.

The role of ultimate Zionist anti-hero, within the Jewish sphere, belonged to Jacob Israel De Haan (illus. 85).[115] In 1919 De Haan was the first Jew from the Netherlands to emigrate to the Jewish settlement in Palestine. Before this he had gained fame in a number of disparate quarters: born the son of a cantor in the northern Netherlands, he became an active anarchist and socialist while pursuing a career as a writer and poet. He wrote the first widely read homoerotic fiction in Europe, which threw his political career into turmoil. He also was a lawyer and legal scholar, now recognized for pioneering the application of semiotics to the law.[116] In the wake of the First World War he turned to Zionism, then religious Zionism, and moved to Palestine.

Upon settling in Palestine, he grew disenchanted with Zionism and became a disciple of the anti-Zionist, ultra-Orthodox Jerusalem rabbi, Haim Sonnenfeld. Sonnenfeld was the leader of the ultra-Orthodox 'Haredim' who embraced De Haan and made him the 'foreign minister' of their party. De Haan also took a lead role in criticizing Zionist authorities before the British Mandatory power and the foreign press. Among the fascinating people with whom he was in contact were his avant-garde novelist sister, Carry Van Bruggen, and his fellow journalist Leopold Weiss, who became the important Muslim scholar and publicist, Muhammed Asad.

De Haan was murdered under mysterious circumstances in 1924, as he was about to embark on negotiations with leading Arab political figures. At that time, it was alleged that his murder was perpetrated by Arabs who were infuriated by his liaisons with Arab boys; now it is assumed that he was murdered by a group of Zionists, who later would be central to the formation of both the Israeli army and the Israeli state. De Haan's political goals were to circumvent and undermine the Zionists, in order to secure a refuge for ultra-Orthodox, anti-Zionist Jewry under the auspices of an Arab commonwealth. At the time of his murder, he also was about to expose a web of corruption and intrigue – including attempted murder – among the Zionists. He was, in essence, the first Jewish victim of a Jewish political murder in modern times: killed because he was beyond the pale of political and sexual respectability. His legacy is of continuing significance for anti-Zionist Orthodox Jews, secular critics of nationalist excesses, and the gay avant-garde worldwide.[117]

3 Greater Deviations

However wide the gap between Zionism's aspirations and its actual power in the West, it was the most international and cohesive of late nineteenth- to mid-twentieth-century Jewish movements. Not surprisingly, though, other political currents could boast intercontinental connections.[1] There were several significant individuals who provided links between Eastern Europe and the New World. Particularly notable were those who had come to New York after a period of activism in London, such as the pioneering socialist Aahron Lieberman;[2] the anarchist editor and orator Saul Janowsky;[3] John Dyche, who became a leader of the International Ladies' Garment Workers' Union;[4] Morris Feinstone, head of the United Hebrew Trades, who had passed through both France and England;[5] and the trade unionist Sidney Hillman (see illus. 17) who later served in the Roosevelt administration.[6] Although it is legendary that the American (non-Jewish) journalist John Reed was important enough to Russian communism to be buried in the Kremlin, at least one formidable player on the American Yiddish labour scene, Isaac Hourwich, was accorded a hagiography in *The Great Soviet Encyclopedia*.[7]

To be sure, Zionism possessed distinctive characteristics in each nation, but it also could boast a common core of leaders and principles, despite the unbinding nature of commitment to the cause. Along with Zionism's ubiquity was its penchant for adaptation to local circumstances and the desires of its constituents. It promised a great deal but, aside from asking for money, it did not demand much from either its imagined Jewish constituents or the countries of the West. The great exception, of course, was the appeal for the right and means to settle Palestine. Although the goal of the Zionist movement was ostensibly Jewish separatism, it appeared willing (even if it was not emphatic about it) to accommodate itself to existing Western power structures, although there was tension, particularly between Zionists and government authorities in Britain, due to the ambivalence of the Mandatory power in Palestine. And as part of the unfolding tragedy of the destruction of European Jewry, after 1933 Zionists would suffer and die under the German National Socialists,[8] despite the limited co-operation achieved through the controversial 'Transfer Agreement'.[9] But outside Britain and Palestine the relative lack of open conflict between Zionists and governmental authorities is striking. In large part this was the pattern that had been set by Herzl and the First Congress, when Herzl pledged, in the name of his movement, that to be a Zionist was mutually compatible with loyalty to one's 'home' nation. Zionism's priority was to alter power relations in the Middle East so as to bring to life its 'national home' – as well as to establish and perpetu-ate Zionist hegemony in the Jewish world. Regarding relations between Jews and the state per se, outside Austria and Poland,[10] Zionists were relative latecomers to the notion of exercising influence at home. Before the First World War this was one of the burning ques-tions of the movement: should Zionists take part in local or national politics, as Zionists? Over time, Zionists did assert themselves outside the realm of Zionist institutions and organizations – in conducting refugee relief during and after the First World War, and in the munici-pal affairs of cities such as in Vienna and New York. Many proved themselves adept at and committed to promoting Jewish welfare and human rights writ large.

If Zionism, then, represents the most accommodationist of the Jewish political alternatives – seen from the West, that is – the move-ment that scraped most harshly against the grain was Jewish anarchism. By definition it seems to defy classification. Anarchism, perhaps due to enduring stereotypes, has received relatively little scholarly attention in Jewish history;[11] it was nevertheless a significant part of the Jewish political landscape in major metropolitan centres, especially London. Paul Avrich, a leading historian of anarchism, states that Jewish anarchism was 'one of the largest and most active of the national elements which made up the anarchist movement in the United States'.[12] In the mid-1880s, it could be argued that 'the main strength of the anarchist movement', general and Jewish, 'lay in Chicago'.[13] Anarchism, rather than simply meaning chaos, was made up of three 'contending schools': 'Anarcho-syndicalism, which pinned its hopes on the labour movement, on workers' committees and work-ers' control of industry'; 'individualist anarchism, which was suspicious of all organizations, fearing that they inevitably give rise to hierarchies, leaders and bosses', emphasizing instead

personal autonomy [and] the right of voluntary co-operation, with with-drawal from groups and associations at the individual's own desire. A third major school was communist anarchism, most closely associated with Prince

Kropotkin. This school wanted to combine syndicalist, individualist and collectivist ideas into territorial communes in which workers, farmers and intellectuals would live together in harmony, alternating their jobs and living in relatively small, integrated communities,

with property held in common.[14] Jewish anarchists were perceived as leaders in each stream.

Ironically, Jewish anarchism in both London and New York was in large measure spurred and represented non-Jews. In London anarchism's leading light was German-born Rudolf Rocker, who also was a trade unionist (illus. 86).[15] The peak of Rocker's popularity was during the famous tailors' strike of 1912, when along with Philip Kaplan he was seen as brilliantly directing the workers' tactics.[16] One of his colleagues recalled that 'Born of a Protestant father and a Catholic mother, [Rocker] did not know a word of Yiddish.' Upon moving to the East End of London, in the process of learning the *mame loshn*, 'he became one of the great writers in the Yiddish language'.[17] However, Rocker was not a complete Yiddish novice in Whitechapel; in 1895 in Liverpool he founded and edited a Yiddish

86 Rudolf Rocker (1873–1958): Rocker had a long and distinguished career in left-wing politics and Yiddish culture. Frontispiece of Rocker, *Hinter shekhege druht un grates* (1927).

87 Johann Most (1846–1901): Shown here on the cover of a 1906 Yiddish pamphlet about 'Communist Anarchism', Most is treated sympathetically in Rudolf Rocker's informative biography.

monthly of social theory, named for the naturalist novel of Émile Zola, *Germinal*. His reputation, however, would develop mostly during his editorship of *Der arbeter fraynd* in London. Although this paper and its related club were shut down during the First World War, Rocker continued to do 'a remarkable job of education and organization among the Jewish workers'[18] when he was not in prison or in forced exile from Britain. Although it is no surprise that Rocker translated the works of Gorky, Kropotkin, Nietzsche and Marx into Yiddish, he also was the Yiddish translator of a tract on economics by Zionist Max Nordau.[19] In Rocker's crowd, Nordau was no less than arch-reactionary. Rocker was apparently sensitive to the fact that Nordau, the Zionist, propounded an economic theory of co-operativism not that alien from his own.

Compared to Rocker, another Gentile, Johann or John Most (illus. 87), was a more detached 'apostle of anarchism to the Jewish immigrants' in New York.[20] Still, his influence was unique and enduring.[21] Emma Goldman recalled that in 1896

I heard the first great anarchist speaker – the inimitable John Most. It seemed to me then, and for many years after, that the spoken word hurled forth among the masses with such wonderful eloquence, such enthusiasm and fire, could never be erased from the human mind and soul. How could any one of all the multitudes who flocked to Most's meetings escape his prophetic voice! Surely they had but to hear him to throw off their old beliefs, and to see the truth and beauty of anarchism![22]

Most, whose theatrical aspirations were thwarted by a facial deformity which he later tried to cover with a beard,[23] never immersed himself in the world of Yiddish, as did Rocker. But he nevertheless became the mentor of Goldman, Alexander Berkman and numerous lesser-knowns. Most's newspaper, *Freiheit*, in German, had a tremendous influence on Jewish anarchism in the United States.[24] When publicly charged in 1901 with 'printing an inflammatory article in his paper, *Die Freiheit*, on the eve of the assassination of President McKinley', he was defended by Morris Hillquit and the *Forward*.[25] Although Most is primarily remembered for advocating terrorism as a necessary expedient of radical politics, and for his undermining of respect for traditional Judaism,[26] earlier evaluations see his role as more pronounced and complex.[27] For instance, the evolution of his radical-ism could be traced to his encounter with Russian Jewish radicals in London.[28] His followers most likely understood that his contempt for Judaism was not nearly as disdainful as his attitude towards Christianity, as a fount of exploitation of the working class.

In Germany the leading Jewish anarchist, who preached a utopian, non-violent anarchism, was Gustav Landauer (illus. 88). Landauer, too, had myriad Jewish connections, including ties to Zionists – notably Martin Buber. His influence resonated in the life and works of Buber, Hans Kohn, Rudolf Kayser, Leo Loewenthal, George Mosse, Manes Sperber, Gershom Scholem, Walter Benjamin, Ernst Bloch and Ernst Toller. Landauer's fellow anarchist Erich Muehsam gained fame for ridiculing Jewish solidarity by saying that 'We Jews have as much and as little in common with one another as "we Germans", as "we French", as "we riders in the same bus"!' Yet Muehsam, too, publicly endorsed Buber's Zionism as 'appropriate for us Jews'.[29] James Joll summarizes Landauer's career thus: 'In April 1919, he became the People's Commissar of Culture in the short-lived Councils Republic of Bavaria; he was murdered by the Army on 2 May 1919, after the defeat of the revolution in Munich. His profoundly original works have been defined . . . as "an anarchist form of Jewish messian-ism".'[30] Landauer would not enjoy the mass appeal of the figures on the street in London and New York, but he would exert an intellectual influence of significance until the generation of the Jewish 'New Left' in Europe and the United States.[31]

Rather than migrating from East to West, anarchism tended to

88 Gustav Landauer
(1870–1919): A utopian
humanist who ventured
into the political breach
and gave his life to the
cause, Landauer's ethical
and intellectual influence
endured. Frontispiece of
Landauer, *Oyfruf tsum
sotsializm* (1920).

spread from London to the shtetl; as one writer recalled, it was

> brought over into our town [Ruzhanoi or Ruzhany, in the province of Grodno in today's Belarus, a shtetl of 6,000] from Bialystok, . . . straight from London, where anarchist theories, or rather moods, still had adherents among footloose Jewish immigrants. One might say that London was the mother of Jewish anarchism in Russia. In our area anarchism was an occasional peculiarity. The first anarchists who drifted to Bialystok from London found their most attentive listeners among the tannery workers. Theirs was a highly skilled and difficult craft.[32]

Ezra Mendelsohn has observed that it was frequently the workers employed in the most hazardous conditions, including tannery workers, who were drawn to radical politics.[33] '"Direct action" appealed to many of them and was conveniently interpreted as a license to seize wealthy individuals and hold them for ransom.'[34] Perhaps there has been less romanticization of the Jewish experience in London's East End, as opposed to New York's Lower East Side, partly because of the pre-eminence of activist-radicals who were 'militantly revolutionary'.

Moreover, such a tendency was made concrete by the 'Siege of Sidney Street' in London in 1911, which was 'given a lurid treatment in the city's press'. It prompted, writes David Cesarani, 'A barrage of hostile comment . . . directed at Jewish immigrants [and] calls for the Aliens Act to be tightened up'.[35]

The London Jewish anarchists' reputation for violence did not prevail in New York. Jewish anarchism was represented in New York primarily through its philosophical newspapers, *Di fraye arbeter shtimme*, which had an unusually long run from 1890 to 1977,[36] and the *Fraygezelshaft*. Among the more colourful proponents of this ideology were Alexander Berkman and Emma Goldman. Berkman's botched attempt to assassinate a steel plant manager in 1892 vitiated his attempt to use himself as a political instrument.[37] Emma Goldman, however much she remains a figure of great interest in retrospect, was not regarded as the chief voice of anarchism, as she was also identified with feminism – apart from the distinctly Jewish sphere. On the Jewish street, however, the figure most associated with anarchism was Saul Janowsky, who did not seem to embody the flamboyance or energy of other anarchists (illus. 89). Hutchins Hapgood wrote that Janowsky was 'a little dark-haired man, with beautiful eyes, and soft-persuasive voice'. He therefore was a fitting leader of the 'anarchists of the ghetto', who were 'a gentle and idealistic body of men'.[38] The bombs they hurled were polemical, rather than destructive of life and limb. Essentially they believed that a humane order would emerge through the abolition of government, which by its very nature tends to oligarchy and corruption. Under Janowsky, anarchism was something to think about; it was more a posture of dignified defiance, as opposed to an ideology or a plan requiring specific policies. Frequently it was referred to as a phase that one passed through, typically as a young person, before deciding on a variety of socialism or Zionism. Figures as diverse as Abraham Cahan, editor of the *Forward*, and Jacob Israel De Haan, a leader of Agudas Yisroel, had tried on anarchism along their journeys.

If the Jewish anarchists in the United States did not appear threatening, the same could not be said for the Jewish communists. Like the anarchists, the communists were also identified with the Yiddish press, namely the daily *Morgn frayhayt*, and its accompanying weekly, *Der Hamer*. At the pinnacle of Jewish communism in the United States was Moissaye J. Olgin (illus. 90), from 1915 until his death immediately before the start of the Second World War. Olgin was born in a shtetl near Kiev, where he had a traditional Jewish upbringing. As a student

89 Saul Janowsky (1864-1939): Soft-spoken and dignified, he was anything but violent. Drawing by S. Raskin.

at the University of Kiev at the turn of the century he joined the underground revolutionary movement, while simultaneously leading a Jewish cadre called 'Frayhayt'. After studying at Heidelberg University Olgin became active in the Vilna Committee of the Bund, and later began a long journalistic career as an editor of *Di arbeter shtimme*. Upon arrival in New York he contributed to the *Forward*. His central role in founding the Workers' Party, or Communists, expectedly brought him into conflict with Cahan and the *Forward* staff. He remained, however, committed to Jewish interests as the chief organizer of the Jewish section of the party.

Olgin was probably best known, however, as a founding editor of the Yiddish daily *Frayhayt*, later the *Morgen frayhayt*, and as a champion of Yiddishism. In an effort similar to Eliezer Ben Yehudah's campaign for Hebrew, Olgin insisted that Yiddish must be the language of the home if it were to survive; he was appalled by the tendency of Jewish intellectuals to use Polish, German and Russian in private.[39] He also served as a prolific cultural and political mediator among the Jews: 'He translated several volumes of Lenin's *Collected Works* from Russian into English; Frederick Engels's *Peasant War in Germany* into Yiddish; John Reed's *Ten Days that Shook the World* from English into Yiddish; a volume of short stories from Polish into Yiddish; two volumes of tales of Mendele Moikher Sforim, the father of Jewish literature, from Hebrew into Yiddish; and Jack London's *Call of the Wild* from English into Yiddish.' There is no doubt that he had an impact well beyond the rolls of the Jewish section of the Communist Party, as over 100,000 persons participated in or observed his funeral in 1939. From the perspective of the Communists, Olgin 'was the outstanding and most beloved figure in the Jewish community'.[40] Certainly the legions staunchly behind Abe Cahan would take issue with this, but the magnitude of his impact faded within a generation.

There is little doubt that Olgin's popularity was constrained by his

90 A portrait of M. Olgin reproduced in at least two pamphlets, as well as in *Morgen frayhayt* and *Der Hamer*. The caption reads: 'The teacher has forever closed his eyes'.

91 Olgin on display after his death. No doubt he intended to be provocative even then; however, he did not remain a subject of discussion for very long. From *M. Olgin Albom* (1941).

harsh stance on Zionism, especially in the wake of the Palestine riots from 1926 onwards,[41] his unabashed adoration of Lenin and his defence of the Nazi–Soviet Non-Aggression Pact – the latter shortly before his death. But there was more to Olgin's 'Jewish communism' than anti-Zionism; he was an outspoken *kempfer* for Yiddish, and the aspect of Leninism he especially prized was that which allowed for the preservation and even nurturing of national minorities within the framework of the Soviet Union. In one of his English columns in the *Morgen frayhayt*, he wrote that:

There is a shelf in the Hall of Science, Literature and the Press in the Soviet Pavilion at the World's Fair. On this shelf there are specimens of books produced in the Soviet Union. As I handled these books one after the other to learn the name of the authors, to scrutinize the paper, the printing and the binding – which, by the way, are excellent – I discovered also a book in Yiddish. It was a volume of folk songs with notes. The book is printed on fine paper with an artistic finish, and the binding is soft leather which it is a joy to touch. The book would be a grand addition to the library of the most fastidi- ous book-collector. It looks like a true work of love: both the text, carefully chosen and arranged, and the exterior bespeak an attitude of great respect and affection for the work at hand.

I held this book in my hands and I thought that this is perhaps the only Yiddish book in the entire Fair. There isn't a single pavilion of any other nation where Yiddish books are shown. There isn't a single nation in the world which has that attitude of deference and fondness for the cultures of minority nationalities which we find in the Soviet Union. On that shelf the Jewish book is not the only representative of a cultural minority; there are books in Georgian, in Armenian, in Uzbek, in Tartar, not to speak of the books in the Ukrainian language which was persecuted and suppressed before 1917.[42]

The Soviet Union, to Olgin, had fostered 'national liberation' on an unprecedented scale; it celebrated, rather than suppressed the plethora of national cultures in its midst. This was the crux of his message delivered to an audience of over 20,000 in New York's Madison Square Garden, on 13 November 1939.[43] Olgin's communism evinced little enthusiasm for Stalinism,[44] and lavished little or no attention on the overthrow of the American or any other government. In fact, the enemies upon whom he fixated seemed to be Jews, above all his counterparts in the Yiddish press, whom he considered anti-Soviet.[45] He relished taunting his Jewish adversaries and flaunting Jewish convention – even posthumously – as his funeral featured the anti-Jewish rite of the open casket (illus. 91). However, Olgin's passion for Yiddish (like that of his enemies) and his rationalization of its place in Jewish life were unequivocal:

There is no way of separating the Jewish people from the Yiddish language. There is no way of separating culture in Yiddish from Jewish life. A young Jewish man or woman wishing to function in the present historical era as part of the progressive forces against anti-Semitism and fascism cannot have the 'I-don't-care' attitude towards the Yiddish language and culture, whether he or she speaks Yiddish or not.[46]

Olgin was not outspoken in praise of the United States, as he was of the Soviet Union. But like the Zionists, the American Jewish communists who hailed Olgin as a hero proudly displayed the American flag along with his portrait (illus. 92). Zionism, socialism and even communism – up to 1939 – were able to coexist comfortably with Americanism, at least among the Jews.

Under the guidance of Olgin, Jewish communist periodicals became the forum for some of the most provocative Jewish art of the early twentieth century. Earlier, *Tsukunft*, from 1892 to 1897, had

92 Displaying the American flag did not seem an empty gesture on the part of American-Jewish Communists. From *M. Olgin Albom* (1941).

93 William Siegel's *The People in the Street* was one of the more militant scenes to appear in the interwar years. From *Der Hamer* (November 1926).

94 Louis Lozowick's *Luna Park* showing one of the ways in which technology was tamed. Cover of *Der Hamer* (August 1926).

featured 'article-length biographies with pen-and-ink drawings of the heroes who struggled for freedom through the ages', including Jews and non-Jews.[47] In addition to portraits of heroic figures, Jewish artists, such as William Gropper, Hugo Gellert, William Siegel (illus. 93) and Louis Lozowick, were published in *Der Hamer*, a Jewish-communist, exclusively Yiddish milieu, a fact which is elusive in their biographies and autobiographies. This was in the 1920s while there was still an opportunity for a marriage of a defiant Yiddishism with communism. Interestingly, there is a substantial body of comment on the Precisionist artist Lozowick, who turned to conventional Jewish motifs later in his career, but it contains practically no acknowledgement of his activity under the auspices of Jewish communism (illus. 94).[48] Lozowick is indicative of the Jewish communists' propensity, shared by many other Jewish political streams, to see technology as a means to attaining a higher life, and having an aesthetic value of its own. His drawings, moreover, should not be wrenched from the Yiddish milieu in which they were embedded (illus. 95).

The choice of language was not then and is rarely now an arbitrary matter: the use of Yiddish was a statement about Jewish identity, as well as an instrument for reaching the masses. The assault on Yiddish

95 A scene by Lozowick evokes the process of building the modern city. Cover of *Der Hamer* (March 1926).

96 William Gropper's depiction of a happy Jewish worker. Cover of *Der Hamer* (May 1926).

was at least threefold. First, it was explicitly attacked by the Zionist champions of Hebraism, in what was a practical struggle in Palestine but mostly a war of ideals in the West. Secondly, it was eroded due to the fact that the upcoming generations were learning their host languages at breakneck rate. And, thirdly, it was scorned as one of the unmistakable stigmas of the Jews' deformed character. Sometimes it was called 'Jewish' and sometimes it was conflated with Hebrew. Social-reformer, journalist and genteel anti-Semite Jacob Riis had derided the 'Hebrew [sic] signs, and incessant chatter in the queer lingo that passes for Hebrew [sic] on the East Side . . .'[49] Lozowick's choice of a supremely 'visible language' as a constituent element of this

97 Winold Reiss's composition showing the young Moses appropriating the Old Testament for Communism. Cover of *Der Hamer* (September 1926).

דער האַמער

work was part and parcel of his radicalism.[50]

Gropper, with whom Lozowick was closely allied, whose work was more directed to political-economic criticism and idealizing the working class rather than glorifying technology, was one of the best-known Jewish artists of his generation. He was a regular contributor to the communist Yiddish periodicals *Frayhayt* and *Der Hamer*. It was here that the 'satirical graphics in the radical Jewish press reached a level of expression that was extreme in its acerbity, though original and polished in its style' (illus. 96).[51] Winold Reiss, in contrast, advocated radicalism through recasting biblical scenes, such as Moses slaying the taskmaster, by way of Primitivist art clearly influenced by Africa (illus. 97).

Another radical whose career spanned Russian revolutionary politics, the Soviet Union and American politics was Isaac Hourwich (illus. 98). As a journalist, scholar, attorney and Russified Jew turned Yiddishist, Hourwich's was a subtle mind dedicated to the Jewish questions of his time. His opinions were based on an immersion in a wealth of raw and scholarly social scientific data and the culture of the masses.[52] Hourwich was among the most important interpreters of political economy for the Jewish immigrants themselves. As an activist he 'belonged to a cohort of

98 Isaac Hourwich (1860–1924): Though Hourwich lost some of his following due to his flirtation with the Bull Moose Party, he was one of the half-dozen most influential forces in Jewish labour politics. Portrait by S. Raskin.

social scientists' who contended that hard-boiled social science must be allied with policy-making.[53] Hourwich advanced a sophisticated, scholarly assessment of the Jewish immigrants' immediate past and present that showed them to be a hugely productive and vital part of the emerging economy. He expanded the horizons of this community through his oratory, official government duty and translations of the works of Karl Marx, among others, into Yiddish.

Hourwich was born into a middle-class family in Vilna in 1860; as a young man he was active in the Russian revolutionary movement and exiled to Siberia in 1881. In 1890 he escaped to the United States, where he soon received a PhD in economics at Columbia University. Upon completing his doctorate in 1893 he became a lecturer in economics and statistics at the University of Chicago. This proved to be a short stay. He was denounced as a Marxist, but in the United States he was a Marxist of the revisionist stripe; he applied Marx critically, not dogmatically.[54] Like many Zionists (whom he would openly support later in life) he also was taken by the ideas of Henry George, although he did not think that George was, properly speaking, 'a socialist'.[55] Hourwich returned to New York in 1900 where he was employed by the federal government as a statistician.

In New York Hourwich was central to a constellation of dynamic leaders who are largely forgotten; when the head of the Cloakmakers' union, Joseph Barondess, was 'attacked by the old guard', he was 'defended by Hourwich'.[56] Along with Barondess and Meyer London, Hourwich 'formed the first unit of the Social Democratic party in New York in 1897'.[57] In New York he practised law and for some time was the law partner of labour leader Louis Miller. Hourwich subsequently went to Washington, where he worked for many years as a government statistician and an expert on mining for the Bureau of the Census.[58] As a result of his government-sponsored research he produced scores of articles and a weighty tome on the economics of immigration to the United States, *Immigration and Labour*. It was through this work that he gained a reputation as an expert in the field. It remains an impressive polemic and piece of scholarship. He exposed the fallacy of accusations that immigrants were taking jobs away from so-called native Americans, that they were a drain on the economy, and that they exhibited an inferior moral constitution – such as through a propensity to criminal behaviour.[59] Hourwich argued that the immigrant masses were increasing the wealth and economic development potential of the nation exponentially; they were helping to provide for greater employment, rather than taking jobs away; and they were no more lawless or measurably immoral in their behaviour than any previous generation of new immigrants. In fact, they constituted less of a social burden than earlier generations of immigrants.[60]

Beginning around 1910 Hourwich enjoined a battle for greater workers' rights, eventually causing him to clash with Louis Brandeis, who nevertheless is – for the most part, correctly – seen as a great champion of Jewish workers, as well as Zionists. It seems that the oblivion to which Hourwich's legacy has been consigned is due, in part, to this bitter fight with Brandeis. Brandeis, however, was on the losing end of his fierce quarrels with Chaim Weizmann, who shunted him from the leadership of world Zionism.

As 'Yitzhok Isaac' Hourwich began to write in Yiddish about 1897, after *Forward* began publication under Abraham Cahan. Since he held a government job, Hourwich could not openly write articles in socialist and even further left papers; a pseudonym was indispensable. He picked a strange pen-name – Yitzhok Ben Arye Zvi Halevi – rife with poetic and animal allusions. In time, Hourwich learned Yiddish well, and became an important Yiddish publicist. Analysing and commenting on American economic and political institutions became his speciality. The vast knowledge of the United States that he had studiously accumulated he mostly related to the thousands of immigrants who kept pouring into the country. He wrote for *Forward*, the anarchist *Fraye arbeter-shtimme*, *Tsukunft*, *Varhayt* and *Der Tog*. It was said that twice in his life – during the First World War and in the wake of the Balfour Declaration – he experienced a Jewish 'reawakening'. Such an evaluation, however, simply conflates sympathy with Zionism and 'Jewishness'. Like Barondess, all of his life was rooted in and devoted to Jewish matters. It is not difficult to see why Hourwich entitled his unfinished autobiography *Memoirs of a Heretic*; it would be especially difficult to sustain his popularity, as he died in 1924, at the height of isolationist hysteria he fought to combat.[61] Isaac Hourwich's ideas were certain to be seen as ill conceived, or even threatening, to those wishing to rationalize an end to an open-door policy towards new immigrants. Indeed, this was the issue that most alienated Jews from the mainstream labour movement. Furthermore, as much as he was renowned as a stylist in Yiddish, his *métier* was analysis. Hourwich did not indulge in melodrama or nostalgia. Historiographically speaking, he was on the wrong side of labour icons such as Brandeis and Samuel Gompers. It was easy to dismiss Hourwich as too sympathetic towards Marxism, but he was in fact a critic of Marxism and was at heart, and in the United States, a revisionist who sought to carve out a place for Jews and workers within the existing system. Despite having his articles appear under the masthead of anarchist and even communist publications,[62] Hourwich's agenda bore a moderate stamp. He asserted 'that the only effective way to resist the steady encroachment of big business was for the socialists to enter into an alliance with middle-class progressive groups, especially the farmers, to elect candidates to office, and thus to carry out a programme of broad social reforms'. Hourwich maintained that the workers would never 'become a majority of the population or be able to take over the government in a constitutional manner'. Thus he committed what was seen as an 'unpardonable act for a Jewish radical of that period. He joined the Theodore Roosevelt

Bull Moose party and, in 1912, ran for Congress in one of the Jewish districts in New York. His candidacy and his speeches caused quite a commotion among his friends and readers . . . He was not elected.'[63] Hourwich's association with Teddy Roosevelt's supporters is more reasonable when one recalls that party's aggressive defence of public welfare and workers' rights, and that one of its luminaries was Arthur Garfield Hays, who was general counsel of the American Civil Liberties Union beginning in 1912.[64]

As early as 1904 Hourwich expressed his unease with the socialist movement over the issue of immigration restriction. Hourwich came down strongly on the side of forbidding restrictions. At the Stuttgart Congress of 1907, Hourwich again found the case for selective exclusion unconvincing.[65] Hourwich was appalled by 'the position of American socialists to immigration'. He painted any such hindrance of immigration, such as those attempted at the conventions in 1908 and 1910, as a betrayal of the principle of class solidarity; such resolutions rendered the socialists' so-called founding tenets a sham.[66]

Although some Jewish radicals may have been incensed at Hourwich's turn to a middle-class party, thousands of Jews were able to sympathize with him. The views espoused by Hourwich and his very symbolic significance are essential if one is interested in understanding how the Jews conceived themselves and their role in their rapidly changing environs.[67] As much as Hourwich clashed with men such as Abraham Cahan and Louis Brandeis, he was nevertheless a vital part of that cohort. In many respects his political programme, a labour alliance with middle-class progressive forces, is that which carried the day in the United States for several decades. He helped set a mould, in American politics, in which one could be Jewish, committed to workers' rights, sensitive to the concerns of other minorities – such as Chinese, Japanese and Indians – who were disenfranchised from the labour and socialist establishments, and still be a member of an established party.

Earlier it was mentioned that Joseph Barondess, whom Hourwich regarded as a close colleague, was memorable for his physical presence (see illus. 16). The Jewish masses were said to have 'followed him unquestioningly and unhesitatingly'. Certainly his leadership was enhanced by the feeling that Barondess

was an imposing figure. Tall, broad-shouldered, and strong, with a shock of black glossy hair, large dark eyes, a sonorous voice and a face which had something of the classical Greek about it, which gave him the appearance of either a priest or a reformed rabbi, and still more of an actor of classical roles . . . He greatly impressed the people, both with his appearance and poise, and also his unique way of talking to them.[68]

Barondess gained fame for leading the first large-scale cloak-makers' strike in 1890. His legend was further galvanized after he was charged with extortion by the manufacturers, but he was released after a few weeks due to the vehemence of public protests. His career as a labour organizer lasted approximately four more years, after an attempt to lead a strike that did not attain its goals. He was a member of the Socialist Labour Party, but by the beginning of the twentieth century his energies were directed increasingly to an insurance business he had founded. His organizational skills and charisma served him well in this, and he prospered. Barondess became interested in Zionism as a means of alleviating the plight of Eastern Jewry, and among other local and national, Jewish and secular offices, he became an honorary vice-president of the Zionist Organization of America and a founding member of the American Jewish Congress. In 1910 he was named the commissioner of the New York City Board of Education. It has been written that 'His career typified that of many immigrants, whose process of integration in the United States was marked by initial disillusionment with American society, socialism, a higher economic status and finally a retreat from radical political activity and a return to the Jewish fold.'[69] But this synopsis is misleading. There is no evidence that in working for Zionism and the American Jewish Congress he meant to disavow his earlier politics. Also, at no point in his life does it seem that he ever strayed from 'the Jewish fold'. Despite his embourgeoisement, he was a leading supporter of Maurice Schwartz's Yiddish Art Theater,[70] seeking not only to keep Yiddish alive, but to improve and broaden its manifestations. More significantly, however, the degree to which he fired the imagination of the Jewish masses as their bold champion – with an aura of sensuality – seems to have been lost. 'The workers loved him . . . Barondess possessed a considerable personal magnetism. A soft good-natured man, it was easy to awaken pity in him, to call forth tears in his eyes, and to get a favor from him . . . His voice alone caused respect. Barondess liked to interlace his speeches with a quotation from the Bible or a saying from the Talmud. I knew many cloakmakers who were literally fascinated by him. They loved him and trembled before him.' Besides being a bridge between trade unionism and Zionism, Barondess was said to be beloved by Hasidim and roughnecks.[71] While he sustained great popularity, there also were those who regarded his transformations with suspicion, possibly seeing more style than substance in his earlier, fiery stages.

In his second place of employment, Morris Hillquit was a shopmate of Barondess; their careers would always be intertwined.[72] Hillquit, a handsome man steeped in both Russian and German culture, would be better remembered than Barondess for leaving his imprint on the labour movement (illus. 99). Hillquit, too, was among those who established the United Hebrew Trades in 1888, while simultaneously assuming a prominent role, notably as a theorist, in the Socialist Party of America from 1900 until his death in 1933. In part he was motivated by a desire to overturn the stigma of the Jew as the instigator and exploiter of the sweating system.[73] Like Hourwich, Hillquit was a Marxist revisionist who abhorred violence, seeking to improve the lot of the working class through electoral politics and popular education.

99 Morris Hillquit (1869–1933): Like many others, Hillquit was remembered for his dignified bearing, culture and oratorical prowess. Along with Meyer, Vladeck and London, and despite their shared radicalism, Hillquit was crucial to the integration of Jewry into the American political mainstream.

Hillquit, too, failed in a bid for elected office, in his case, to be mayor of New York City in 1917.

Hillquit, as mentioned above, was seen as the more 'philosophical' and 'theoretical' in his famous debate with Samuel Gompers. But the incident that led to that exchange was perhaps more significant in the eyes of many Jewish immigrants. It is necessary to revisit the events. Some months before the outbreak of the First World War, on 20 April 1914, an encampment of miners striking against the Colorado Fuel and Iron Company in Ludlow was set ablaze by state troopers on behalf of the mine owners. 'Among those burned to death were eleven children and two women. The miners were immigrants and the strike was called by the syndicalist-oriented Western Federation of Miners, headed by Bill Haywood.' It was recalled to have 'produced a feeling of horror among radical immigrants'. Some months after the tragedy, in an overflowing chamber in the New York City Hall, there was a public cross-examination of John D. Rockefeller Sr., who was 'then a symbol of hard and callous capitalist America, by the president of the AFL, Samuel Gompers, foreign-born and a Jew. The hearing was conducted by the United States Commission on Industrial Relations, headed by Congressman Frank P. Walsh.' Rockefeller, 'surrounded by detectives, had to answer many embarrassing questions. The hall was hushed when Hillquit, in his soft voice, put the final question to Rockefeller, "Do you know that the grass has not yet grown up on the graves of your victims in Ludlow?"'[74]

Even in his young twenties, Hillquit proved to be a powerful figure. 'As soon as he opened his mouth, we opened our eyes and ears. Here was a man with extraordinary powers of speech which enthralled everyone in the audience.'[75] Interestingly, however, as much as Hillquit seemed to be the more 'Jewish' in his famous debate with Gompers, he was faulted in his own time for eschewing the 'special interests' of the Jewish East Side in favour of 'the interests of the working class' writ large, and he was taken to task in the Yiddish press for shirking his Jewish responsibilities.[76] There is no doubt, however, about his inclusion in the pantheon of Jewish labour icons; he attempted to extend his politics beyond the Jewish sphere, but always while rooted among the Yiddish-speaking masses.[77] Ironically, Hillquit was the famous ghost writer, 'Psalmist', who 'denounced capitalism and the world's many evils' in the pages of the *Tsukunft*.[78] It would be virtually impossible to be more anti-Jewish in a Jewish sort of way. Despite what was seen as the problematic nature of his commitment to fellow Jews in the eyes of some critics, Hillquit emerged as among the 'best, morally and intellectually, that Jewish socialism had to offer'.[79]

Meyer London (illus. 100) is the labour leader, attorney and politician most often associated with Hillquit. There is no doubt that, of the two, he was perceived as the more dedicated to Jewish issues. In the late 1890s, London established his reputation at the well-attended Friday evening, English-language meetings of the Hebrew Institute (later known as the Educational Alliance). Audiences 'were impressed by his reasoning, and he soon became popular as a debater'. Like others who dissented from Daniel De Leon in the early phase of Jewish labour organization, 'London resigned from the Socialist Labour party, on whose ticket he had already run for Assemblyman in 1896, and plunged into the work of building up the new socialist body.' Hourwich, Barondess and London 'appeared at the convention of the Jewish insurgents of the Socialist Labour party, July 31, 1897, to

100 Meyer London (1871–1926): Unquestionably a favourite son of New York's Lower East Side, he did not need a beard to be identified as Jewish.

appeal for their affiliation with the new party. To overcome the objections of many delegates that the Debs movement lacked a clearcut socialist thought, London emphasized the American character of the new party and the personality of its leader.'[80] Only a month after Jewish socialism in the United States was assuming a definite form, the Zionist movement would set a mould for itself in Basel.[81]

London became the sacrificial lamb of the Socialist Party as its regular candidate for the New York State Assembly; at that time the socialists were not regarded as serious contenders. London did, however, make a name for himself as an orator. He was known for not striving for pathos in his speeches, and for adopting a serious, confident, analytic manner, usually speaking in English. It was said that he 'was the only Jewish Socialist to venture into the outlying districts of the East Side, inhabited by Germans and Irish usually unfriendly to Jews. His courage, sincerity and eloquence overcame their prejudice, and they stopped to listen to him.'[82] At the United States Socialist Party Congress of 1910, London defended Asian immigration and anti-discrimination, saying that

One of the painful things in life that I have been acquainted with is the murder of Chinese by thugs and ruffians. When you say, 'we will exclude people because they are Japanese and because they are Chinese and because they are Hindus you violate the Decalogue, one of the elementary principles of international Socialism . . .'[83]

Similar to Hillquit, Meyer London also found his calling as a needle-trade organizer in New York; similar to Hourwich, he was a leading labour lawyer and indefatigable fighter for unrestricted immigration.[84] Indeed, it was the latter issue, immigration, which tended to divide the leadership of the United Hebrew Trades from the American Federation of Labour. 'It would take several decades', Irving Howe wrote, 'before this clash between the Jewish socialist union leaders and the official AFL leadership came, not to an end, but at least to a point where it could be quietly contained.' Furthermore, Howe noted in 1975, the historiography on the labour movement did not reflect this schism,[85] and twenty years hence few scholars have reopened this question.[86]

London succeeded where both Hourwich and Hillquit failed: he did gain elected office, serving as a member of the US House of Representatives beginning in 1914. 'That election night', Irving Howe wrote,

there occurred one of those emotional outpourings which seems to have been a profound need of East Side, perhaps of all Jewish, life. Crowds started gathering at dusk on Rutgers Square, facing the Forward building; at two in the morning, recalls an old Socialist, 'Tammany leaders conceded London's election. Joy broke out among the assembled mass. Men sang and danced . . . London was brought to the square at four in the morning to head an impromptu demonstration.' The writer still remembers the march over the streets at early dawn; M. Zametkin [a venerable comrade] speaking from the balcony of the Forward, lifting his hands to the rising sun, exclaiming, 'Perhaps the sun will shine on the East Side from now on.' The following Sunday the Socialists held an overflow celebration at Madison Square Garden, and London spoke simply and modestly: 'I do not expect to work wonders in Congress. I shall, however, say a new word and I shall accomplish one thing that is not on the platform of the Socialist Party. I hope that my presence will represent an entirely different type of Jew from the kind that Congress is accustomed to see.' It was, in good part, for this last remark that the East Side had chosen Meyer London.[87]

Like Hillquit, London's reputation suffered due to his opposition to American entrance into the First World War, and his reluctance formally to endorse Zionism probably cost him a re-election victory.[88] Whereas Barondess turned his talents for organization and fundraising to Zionism, beginning around 1903 London focused his energy on augmenting the fortunes and moral support of the Bund in Russia – which contributed to a reversal of fortune in his own career.[89]

As his election victory was seen as one of the more noteworthy public rites of the Lower East Side, so was his funeral: 'On June 10, 1926 five-hundred thousand people, friends and foes, crowded the sidewalks of the East Side to show their affection and respect for the man who had lived and grown among them, scold though he had sometimes seemed. The hearse that bore his remains to their final resting place was followed by fifty-thousand men, women, and children from a wealth of diverse nationalities, religions, social positions, and political affiliations . . . "For six hours", one New York newspaper reported the next day, "the East Side put aside its duties, pressing or trivial, to do honor to its dead prophet."'[90] Although he was not a member of the Democratic or Republican Party, London moved from the margins into the political mainstream. Certainly his impact on labour relations, which would be carried on by unions and non-governmental organizations, was profound.

Another figure who successfully entered the secular political arena without masking or sacrificing his *yiddishkayt* was Baruch Charney Vladeck, seen as one of the Jewish labour movement's 'most brilliant and devoted generals' (illus. 101).[91] He tended to be portrayed in decisive-looking poses, featuring his dark features and thick hair (illus. 102). Baruch Charney Vladeck was born in Minsk province, Russia;

before immigrating to the United States he had been active in the revolution of 1905, dedicating himself primarily to the Bund – which earned him three prison terms. He had also embarked on a career in Yiddish letters in the 'old country', the beginning of a formidable contribution in terms of quality and scope of intellectual interests.[92] Vladeck was recognized as one of the most outstanding practitioners of 'the New Yiddish Literature'.[93] Upon arrival in New York in 1908 his rise in the Jewish labour ranks was swift; he was praised, in a front-page article in the *Forward*, as 'the young Lassalle',[94] and immediately commenced a North American-wide speaking tour. There was no sign of disappointment; Vladeck was hailed as a gifted and engaging speaker. He held the crucial post of city editor for the *Forward* beginning in 1916, and became its business manager in 1918. He served as an alderman of New York City from 1918 to 1921, as a representative of the Socialist Party. In 1934, 'when he was appointed to the New York City Housing Authority, he made himself an expert on the technical as well as social aspects of Housing'.[95] The housing co-operatives he inspired came to be known as 'Vladeck Houses'.[96] These are among the few public structures in the United States that clearly exhibit Jewish motifs.[97] 'His activities in the ORT [Organization for Rehabilitation

101 Vladeck as a New York City Alderman. From Vladeck, *Vladeck in lebn un shafen* (1936).

through Training[98]], the Jewish Labour Committee, the Hebrew Immigrant Aid Society, [public radio] Station WEVD and other significant organizations gave him a broad view of human relations and needs. At the very end of his career he was Majority Leader in the New York City Council, where his leadership made him a distinguished figure in the city's life.'[99] Vladeck is a leading example of the merger between politics and poetics on the Jewish street; some of his colleagues questioned 'whether his greater gift might not have been in literature' as opposed to politics.[100] He was lauded, as well, for being able to inform and move the immigrant masses with his speeches.

In Vladeck there was also, for all of his modesty and humility, a pronounced messianic dimension, or at least fascination. He authored a play, in Yiddish, entitled *Moshe Rabeinu*.[101] 'The play, as well as

Vladeck's frequent allusions to Moses in his speeches, clearly indicate a strong sense for the messianic; the lines of a short poem, "The voice that spoke to Moses and Socrates speaks also to me", reveal a religious vein as well.'[102] This concern with Moses might also have been an echo of his youthful enthusiasm for Zionism, which he did not maintain.

Although Vladeck served with passion all the residents of New York he represented, his munificence towards fellow Jews was overwhelming. He was a director of the Hebrew Immigrant Aid Society (HIAS) and a president of ORT; he served on the executive committee of the Yiddish Scientific Institute (now YIVO Institute for Jewish Research), the People's Relief Committee (PRC) (1915–24) and the Joint Distribution Committee. He also helped direct the American Jewish Committee, and he brought anti-Semitism to the forefront of American Federation of Labour concerns.[103] None of these roles were simply nominal; Vladeck was instrumental in all of them.

Although he was not a Zionist, both Vladeck and his brother, the Yiddish poet Shmuel Niger, had gone through a 'Zionist' phase in their early youth before turning to Bundism. Nevertheless, Vladeck was adamant that Jewish political voices other than his own be heard. He gained wide notoriety in 1921, in the midst of his last term on the Board of Aldermen, for defending the right of Chaim Weizmann and Albert Einstein to lobby for Zionism in New York City. At that moment Einstein had agreed to accompany Weizmann, as Weizmann was attempting to gain credibility and support for the new Zionist fundraising and administrative mechanism he had created – over the torrid objections of Brandeis – the Keren Hayesod (Palestine Foundation Fund). A proposal was made by New York Weizmann loyalists to give Einstein and Weizmann the ceremonial keys to the city. As such proclamations were usually pro forma, they were decided by unanimous votes. But an old-guard Republican alderman (Collins) objected, 'saying that he was against giving the two "foreigners" such an honor. Collins recommended himself as a genuine American whose great-great-great grandfather had been secretary to Lord Baltimore.' In the ensuing debate Vladeck gave an address not unlike that of Disraeli in asserting Jewish pride of place in the development of civilization:

Mr. Collins's great-great-great grandfather was a secretary to Lord Baltimore. We know what that meant. He probably polished the lord's boots and served him in many similar ways. The great-great-great grandfather of Weizmann and Einstein was also secretary to the Lord. It was Moses, who carried out God's will and redeemed his people from slavery and later, as a good secretary, inscribed God's Ten Commandments on Tablets.

Vladeck's intercession for the world Zionist president and his most illustrious supporter, Einstein, angered the head of the Bund, Vladimir Medem – who also had recently arrived in New York. Vladeck defended his stance by contending that the alderman's attack was not aimed merely at the Zionists, but at Jewry in total. This type of solidarity, Vladeck reasoned, was essential. 'Vladeck raised the issue to a higher level by affirming that there exists an area of general Jewish interests from which socialists cannot exclude themselves.'[104]

Although he never retreated from his socialist conviction, Vladeck maintained that reform could be generated and sustained only through labour's forging of links with middle-class progressive interests; hence there was a relatively smooth transition, evinced by his family's history, into the Democratic Party. Many writers would comment in later years on American Jewry's abiding links with the Democrats; it was not simply an abstract ideal, but an alliance that was marked by key personalities and relationships, and significant among them was Vladeck, who was a great admirer of Franklin Roosevelt. Among those who were of the utmost significance in integrating Jewry into labour and electoral politics were London, Hillquit, Hourwich and Vladeck, all of whom spoke something of a double language: they articulated their ideas for a general audience, while they simultaneously engaged in a critical discourse that was exclusive to Jewry. They did this not to encourage Jewish separatism, but as a means of recognizing and building on the fact that Jews were not only, in some respects, separate but also distinctive in ways in which Jews should take pride. It is little wonder that Vladeck's funeral in November 1938 caused a huge outpouring on to the streets on New York.

Vladeck's career, brilliant as it was, was in the shadow of the gigantic figure with whom he frequently quarrelled: Abraham Cahan (illus. 103). Cahan still awaits his definitive biography, as the task of comprehending and contextualizing his long and varied career is Herculean. It is widely accepted that Cahan 'seemed in many ways to incarnate the epic Jewish migration from Eastern Europe to America';[105] under his stewardship the *Forward* was hailed as 'the most eloquent expression' of the new Yiddish journalism:

Cahan had come to New York in 1882 at the age of twenty-one, eager for freedom and determined to write. In the ensuing two decades he served an apprenticeship in American living that was to prepare him for his role as editor of the nation's outstanding Yiddish daily. This perceptive Russian intellectual shared in all the experiences of his fellow immigrants: he was factory hand, lecturer, teacher of English, labour organizer, law student, and socialist preacher. But from the outset he cultivated literary ambitions.[106]

103 Abraham Cahan, taut and toughened.

Cahan became the ultimate arbiter of both taste and politics. 'At its peak in the 1920s', the *Forward*'s circulation encompassed '11 local and regional editions, surpassed a quarter of a million and its influence extended to many times that number of people. The *Forward* defended the cause of labour, socialism, humanity, and distinguished Yiddish and other modern literature.'[107] As much as he appeared to epitomize New York's Jews, Cahan's impact reached beyond North America. His novel *Yekel* (1896) was originally published in New York by D. Appleton & Co., and then in London by William Heinemann. Its London appearance was particularly lauded by Israel Zangwill. It was serialized in Yiddish in the *Arbeter tsaytung*, and its Russian translation actually preceded its publication in the original English. It was through the publicity accorded *Yekel* that a drawing of Cahan was first disseminated throughout the United States,[108] although in time his face would be well-known to Jewry worldwide.

Concomitant to his central role in the founding and life of the *Forward*, Cahan also was recognized as critical to the establishment of two of the most significant institutions in American Jewish life, the Arbeter Ring, or Workman's Circle, and the United Hebrew Trades. In 1936, the Workmen's Circle was 'the largest and wealthiest immigrant labour fraternal order, as well as the largest Jewish organization, in America'.[109] Both of these bodies came to be housed under the same roof as the *Forward*, giving the intersecting nexus of Jewish culture and politics a central address. 'It had a large auditorium for meetings and concerts. Built in 1908, it was an audacious project of the *Forward* manager Marcus Jaffee. The high cost of the building nearly wrecked the paper.'[110] It is not surprising, then, that the men identified and glorified as the moving spirits of the *Forward* were also major figures in the other organizations, such as M. Baranov, Abraham Liesen, Benjamin Feigenbaum, Benjamin Schlesinger, Adolf Held, Benzion Maimon, Jacob Reich, L. Fogelman, Leon Kobrin, N. Solowitz and Baruch Charney Vladeck.[111] Although much of the literature focuses on the quarrels, schisms and breakdowns in relations between individuals and organizations, a point that is often eluded is that they were perceived as somehow belonging to each other, despite their differences.

It was the United Hebrew Trades, of which the Workman's Circle was a part, that was seen as the pre-eminent labour body among Jews in the United States, 'the mother organization of all Jewish trade unionists in the United States . . . It entered a field of industrial oppression and chaos, and developed a strong trade union body . . . The widespread unionization of immigrant workers and their integration with the life of American workers stand as the greatest possible testimony to the work of the United Hebrew Trades.'[112] The 'power and prestige' of the UHT, with its 300,000–plus members in the late 1930s, could not be conceived of as separate from the figure of Abraham Cahan, as its fortunes were inextricably tied to the man and his newspaper.[113] In recounting their history in 1938, Cahan loomed as the most formidable galvanizing force:

The Jewish trade union movement of New York may be said to date from July 27th, 1882. On that day, a young Russian intellectual, a former teacher and writer, Abraham Cahan, rose at a socialist meeting of the intelligentsia, and suggested that the Jewish workers be addressed in Jewish [Yiddish], not

Russian or German. The proposal astounded the intellectuals, who had remained cut off from the masses precisely because they had made no serious effort to bridge the linguistic gap between themselves and the workers. But Cahan's suggestion was followed, more perhaps in an experimental frame of mind than in conviction. Although the final fruits were not to come until 1888, when the UHT was established, the intervening six years were full of extraordinary activity, developing a whole movement towards what might be called popular education. The Jewish workers were addressed in their own tongue, in a simple and unassuming manner, so that they gradually got over their understandable fear of the 'highbrow' ideas of the 'Deitsche' and 'Russische' intellectuals. Agitation for trade union and socialist principles was received with interest. A whole series of educational clubs and organizations was founded. In 1884, the Russian–Jewish Workers' Alliance was formed, its purpose being to hold lectures and meetings in Jewish [Yiddish] for the spread of socialist thought. In 1885, the Labour Lyceum began sending out Jewish speakers. Another body set up at that time was the Jewish Workers' Alliance, an amalgam of the Russian, Hungarian and Galician Jews, established for the spread of socialist ideas and for the founding of a paper. The Jewish Workers' Alliance enjoyed an active but very short life, for two years later it was split by the old controversy over the place of politics in the trade unions. Of the two resultant wings, one became the Anarchists under Janowsky and Zolataroff, while the other became the powerful Branch 8 of the Socialist Labour Party. Cahan and Michael Zametkin were the leading spirits of Branch 8.[114]

As much as Cahan's advocacy parallels the rise of the United Hebrew Trades, he also helped define two central aspects of its programme: the aversion to communism and the gradual warming of relations with the Zionist movement. His visit to Palestine in 1925 became a legendary turning point for Cahan and the *Forward*. There is little possibility that the type of links that were forged between the central bodies of Jewish labour in the United States and Labour Zionism in Palestine could have materialized without Cahan's change of heart. Certainly, had he vigorously opposed the bridge-building with Zionism, such efforts would have experienced far greater difficulty in being achieved. Of course this alliance was aided by the apparent coincidence of interests between Zionism and anti-fascism.

The 1938 annual of the Gewerkschaften of the United Hebrew Trades asserted that

The periodic attacks of anti-Semitism with which our history is punctuated, only make it more imperative for the Jews in America, especially those in the trade unions founded by the United Hebrew Trades, to take stock of the advantages they have gained, and to frame a practical program for applying those advantages to fighting reaction and totalitarianism. The work of the United Hebrew Trades is one more proof that American democracy can and does work. We must realize our assets in order to marshal them against primitivism and unreason. The Jews of the world need our assistance – in Germany, in Central Europe, in Palestine. And we need them in order to assure the triumph of the principles for which we have fought these last fifty years . . . Lastly, we want to call upon all thinking liberals and lovers of freedom to join our crusade against the evils of fascism and super-nationalism.[115]

The organization made specific its perception, if not the reality, of convergence of interests of worldwide Jewish labour movements. Understandably, the United Hebrew Trades' own evaluations did not underscore their bitter strife with the American Federation of Labour, a factor that undoubtedly contributed to cross-party Jewish solidarity. The United Hebrew Trades therefore launched

a standing drive, known as the Gewerkschaften Campaign. This drive raises funds every year for the Histadruth, the Federation of Organized Jewish Workers in Palestine. The UHT set up the American Committee known as the National Labour Committee to work for the establishment of a workers' homeland in Palestine. The organization is nationwide. *The UHT has identified itself with this Palestinian movement, and regards the achievements overseas as a part of its own purposes and ideals.* Since its inception the Gewerkschaften Campaign has raised over two million dollars. Besides raising enormous funds, the Gewerkschaften Campaign does much by way of spreading information concerning Palestine and in stimulating enthusiasm here for the Jewish homeland. It has financed farms and factories in Palestine, and helped to build up resources for recreation, education and health in the new communities. It has far-sightedly regarded Arab enlightenment and improvement as part of its appointed task. The Histadruth, which is the organization in Palestine, regards and always has regarded the Arab masses as brothers to the Jews, and has sought to lift their standards of living and develop their independence and enterprise, so that the two people may dwell in civilized harmony and equality. The UHT, profiting by its experience with American-Jewish immigration and its success in establishing economic equality between the incoming Jews and the 'native' Americans, believes that the same principle can and will work in Palestine, where the Jews are in the position of technical superiority. Despite all the fortunes, or misfortunes of impending European wars, despite the complicating factors of external diplomacies in Palestine, the Histadruth and the UHT believe that Palestine can accommodate the Jews and the Arabs peaceably if the Arab masses are freed from the oppression of their own overlords, and learn to regard themselves as having rights equal to those of the more enterprising Jews. This is a highly democratic and fraternal principle, one which should be the basis of all contemporary international trade relations; it must be the basis of any decent and enduring civilization. Since it is a principle under attack just now from fascist sources, the Histadruth in Palestine and the UHT in America show the courage of conviction by unremitting efforts to make it succeed in the face of very grave obstacles. The UHT has also been a mainstay of the People's Relief Committee, which co-operated with the Joint Distribution Committee for relief of war victims abroad after the World War. [Emphasis added.][116]

On the British scene the politics of Jewish labour also became inter-mingled with Zionism and anti-fascism. There was, however, no equivalent to Abe Cahan and the *Forward* for setting or measuring the pulse of Jewish politics.[117] In part, this is due to the smaller scale of British Jewry, as well as the fact that the Jewish labour movement in Britain, especially among garment workers, was divided between London and Leeds. Indeed, as Anne Kershen has shown, Leeds was so significant that its workers constituted the majority of 'trade unionists who came together in 1915 to create the United Garment Workers' Trade Union'.[118] Hence, a British union leader like Joseph Finn did not enjoy the same popularity as a Barondess or Hillquit. Moreover, American Jews (and non-Jews) seem to have developed more of a toler-ance for Jewish Jews in their public sphere than did their British counterparts.

Still, there were a few individuals who represented the origins and aspirations of Anglo–Jewry who were not part of the older, established elite. The best-known Jewish political figure with immediate ties to the immigrant generation was Manny (Emanuel) Shinwell, who was born in London's East End, but grew up in Glasgow (see illus. 26). His portrait gives little hint of his reputation and self-image as both an expert boxer and a streetwise scrapper. Shinwell, the first Jew to sit for Labour in Parliament, who ended his hundred-plus years in the House of Lords, served in MacDonald's pre-Second World War cabinets and later was the minister of mines. Beginning life on the docks, and as a trade union organizer, Shinwell was not a part of Jewish culture as were figures such as Barondess, Cahan, Vladeck, Hillquit and London in New York. Perhaps more importantly, he was a solitary and quirky figure, apparently not a part of a visible Jewish cohort.

Despite the fact of his Jewishness being more a matter of back-ground, as opposed to an urgent concern, it was Shinwell who provided one of the most memorable moments of Jewish self-assertion in Western politics in the years before the Holocaust. While addressing the House of Commons on the subject of foreign affairs, another MP, Commander Bower, insulted him with the epithet: 'Go back to Poland!' In the wake of a demand for an apology by one of his colleagues, Shinwell approached Bower and 'struck him on the side of his jaw, which seemed to hurt him'. What made this all the more dramatic was that Commander Bower was claimed to be a former heavy-weight boxing champion of the Royal Navy. Shinwell, too, had been a boxer in his youth, and was deeply influenced by the fighter Robert

Fitzsimmons. It is no accident that both his early pugilistic career and the Bower incident are alluded to in the title of one of Shinwell's published memoirs: *Lead with the Left*.[119]

Although their man did not share Shinwell's taste for boxing, the supporters of the Liberal MP for Whitechapel (1931–5), Barnett (Barney) Janner (illus. 104), lent their representative a tough, fighting motto: 'Vote, vote, vote for Barney Janner/Kick old Hall in the eye/When he comes to the door/We will punch him in the jaw/And he won't come voting anymore!'[120] Janner was not seen as a man of the people to the same extent as was New York's Meyer London, but he was able to address his constituents in fine Yiddish,[121] and he was perceived as a staunch upholder of Jewish rights. Janner, as opposed to Shinwell, was expressly committed to Zionism; both, nevertheless, saw themselves as guarantors of Jewish well-being. They assumed that attention to local and even international Jewish affairs was among their duties and, like their US brethren, sincerely believed that their opinions and proposals would matter, if need be.

The most glorious moment of pre-Second World War Anglo–Jewish history was 'the Battle for Cable Street' of 1936 (illus. 105), in which Jews fought British fascists in the East End. In this episode there was no single figure identified with leading the charge or inspiring the Jewish masses, and the evolving mythology has stressed the selfless, sacrificial character of the Jews' courageous demonstration. Ironically, some of the figures associated with confronting Oswald Mosley's Blackshirts were tied to the Jewish criminal underworld, such as John 'Southpaw Cannonball' Lee, the grandfather of the Kray brothers,[122] and Jack Spot. 'According to Spot he approached Mosley's leading bodyguard, a six-foot-six all-in wrestler, "Roughneck", and felled him with a chair leg filled with lead. It was a story on which he traded for the remainder of his working life.'[123] If there was any bridge between the

104 Barnett Janner (1892–1982): Surrounded by a throng of supporters.

105 Newspaper photograph of 'The Battle of Cable Street', seen as a selfless assertion of Jewish rights and pride; the event is memorialized in a little-visited mural.

Jewish tough-guy crooks who stood their ground against Mosley, and upstanding politicians, it is the veneration reserved for 'messianic' Jewish fighters like Kid Lewis and Kid Berg.[124]

Overall, Western Jews' political imagination stressed the notion that they were standing up for themselves and practising a politics of conscience. Their self-portrayals also underscored the contradiction that they wished both to 'fit in' and to 'stand out'; they insisted that they were 'different' but also 'no different', and should be respected from both perspectives.[125] In harbouring and cultivating such contradictions they were pioneering a new orientation to politics and culture that would come to be seen as typical, the very hallmark of ethnic politics, in the modern world.

Epilogue

The style and substance of the face that Western Jews presented to themselves, from the fin-de-siècle to the beginning of the Second World War, conveyed the impression that they were capable of taking matters of concern to them, and to the Jewish world at large, into their own hands. Jews were spectators, if not participants, in their own triumphalist myth. Modern society and its concomitant media quickened the process. It would be an exaggeration to claim that the celebrities and their cults presented here constituted the 'new rabbis of liberty'.[1] But they gave answers, and the models of their own lives to emulate, to Jews seeking self-expression, political voices, and interpretations of their role in the world – as part of a process of secularization of Jewish authority in the twentieth century. If these leaders who had emerged from the Jews could not radically change the world, they could nevertheless have input, and some effect, as Jews. This often was attainable by virtue of their being Jews attached to larger entities, such as Jewish socialists, Jewish Americans, and members of the Anglo–Jewish community. Robert Briscoe, the Irish nationalist who became the first Jewish mayor of Dublin, was quoted as defining himself as 'an Irish Jew – one of the lepre-cohens'.[2] The development of American and British Jews' representation among their own people, in the political and symbolic senses, was part of a process of coming of age. It also constituted a manifestation of collective self-esteem, which must be seen as inextricably bound with the achievement of civic security and material success. Jewish peoplehood evolved as Jews integrated in the West; it did not simply diminish or disappear. The assemblage of Jewish notables, of varying political camps tied to institutions that came more and more to overlap, reinforced the myth of mutual accountability and solidarity among the Jews.

The growth of politicized picturing of Jewry seemed to testify that Jews possessed beauty, dignity, and worth – inner and outer. This was not simple mimicry of the Gentiles. In this process Jews were prized and praised for their rootedness in and ongoing commitments to the

Jewish world, however much there was ambivalence towards supposedly outmoded forms of Jewish life. Significantly, it was virtually impossible, as in the larger cultures they would have been aware, to be too intellectual, or too aggressive for the sake of good causes; seemingly 'Jewish' traits were connoted as overwhelmingly positive. These forces were seen as part of what had earned their inclusion into the West without disgraceful sacrifices.

An investigation of Jewish visual politics from the turn of the century through the 1930s may prompt a reinvestigation of the impact of the Holocaust on Jewish life outside the killing ground. This study suggests that the degree of Jewish integration in the West by the time of the outbreak of war in 1939, from the Jews' own perspective, was greater than that which is typically assumed. Therefore, the paralysis and shock of the Holocaust may represent an even deeper trauma, such as has been noted by cultural historians, due to the discrepancy between the Jews' ineffectiveness in the face of the Nazis versus their view that they had, in many respects, achieved substantial status in Western politics, as Jews. Nevertheless, the assertion of self-conscious Jews into the breach of culture and politics in the West would remain a persistent feature of their lives in these societies, and would help pave the way for a politics of inclusion that would be dear to countless others.

References

Introduction

1 Among the notable exceptions are Jack Kugelmass, 'Jewish Icons: Envisioning the Self in Images of the Other', in *Jews and Other Differences: The New Jewish Cultural Studies*, ed. Jonathan Boyarin and Daniel Boyarin (Minneapolis and London, 1997), pp. 30–53; Michael P. Steinberg, 'Aby Warburg's Kruezlingen Lecture: A Reading' (interpretative essay) following Aby M. Warburg, *Images from the Region of the Pueblo Indians of North America*, trans. and ed. Michael P. Steinberg (Ithaca and London, 1995), pp. 59–114; see also Richard I. Cohen, 'Jewish Art in the Modern Era', in *The Modern Jewish Experience: A Reader's Guide*, ed. Jack Wertheimer (New York and London, 1993), pp. 228–41.

2 Richard I. Cohen, *Jewish Icons: Art and Society in Modern Europe* (Berkeley, 1998); Norman L. Kleeblatt, ed., *Too Jewish?: Challenging Traditional Identities* (New York and New Brunswick, NJ, 1996).

3 Walter Benjamin, 'The Work of Art in the Age of Mechanical Reproduction', in *Illuminations*, ed. Hannah Arendt, trans. Harry Zohn (New York, 1968), pp. 217–51. The literature on Benjamin is immense; among the best guides are the introduction by Anson Rabinbach to *The Correspondence of Walter Benjamin and Gershom Scholem, 1932–1938*, trans. Gary Smith and Andre Lefevere (New York, 1989), and Michael P. Steinberg, ed., *Walter Benjamin and the Demands of History* (Ithaca and London, 1996).

4 A great stride in this direction has been achieved in Linda Nochlin and Tamar Garb, eds, *The Jew in the Text: Modernity and the Construction of Identity* (London, 1995); see also Matthew Frye Jacobson, *Special Sorrows: The Diasporic Imagination of Irish, Polish, and Jewish Immigrants in the United States* (Cambridge, MA, 1995) and Jacobson, *Whiteness of a Different Color: European Immigrants and the Alchemy of Race* (Cambridge, MA, 1998), pp. 171–99.

5 George L. Mosse, *The Crisis of German Ideology* [1964] (New York, 1981); Mosse, ed., *Nazi Culture: Intellectual, Cultural, and Social Life in the Third Reich* (New York, 1966); Robert S. Wistrich, *A Weekend in Munich: Art, Propaganda, and Terror in the Third Reich* (London, 1995); Peter Adam, *Art as Politics in the Third Reich* (New York, 1992).

6 Geoffrey Alderman, *The Jewish Community in British Politics* (Oxford, 1983), p. 66; David Feldman, *Englishmen and Jews: Social Relations and Political Culture, 1840–1914* (New Haven, 1994). For an alternative reading, downplaying the presence of anti-Semitism, see W. D. Rubinstein, *A History of the Jews in the English-Speaking World: Great Britain* (Basingstoke, 1996), pp. 94–363.

7 Hutchins Hapgood, *The Spirit of the Ghetto* [1902], ed. Moses Rischin (Cambridge, MA, 1967), p. 5.

8 Jacob Riis, *How the Other Half Lives: Studies Among the Tenements of New York* [1901] (New York, 1971), p. 38.

9   *Ibid.*, p. 85.

10 Ellen Condliffe Langemann, *A Generation of Women: Education in the Lives of Progressive Reformers* (Cambridge, MA, and London, 1979), p. 75.

11 See Lillian D. Wald, *The House on Henry Street* (New York, 1915); Wald, *Windows in Henry Street* (Boston, 1934).

12 John Tagg, *The Burden of Representation: Essays on Photographies and Histories* (Amherst, MA, 1988), pp. 133, 117–19.

13 See Eleanor H. Adler, 'Child Flower-Makers in New York Tenements', *Child Labor Bulletin*, III/4 (February 1915), pp. 17–18.

14 Riis, *How the Other Half Lives*, p. 89.

15 Steven E. Aschheim, *Brothers and Strangers: East European Jews in German and German–Jewish Consciousness, 1800–1923* (Madison, WI, 1982); Jack Wertheimer, *Unwelcome Strangers: East European Jews in Imperial Germany* (New York and Oxford, 1987); Jonathan Boyarin, *Polish Jews in Paris: The Ethnography of Memory* (Bloomington, 1991); Michael Marrus, *The Politics of Assimilation: A Study of the French Jewish Community at the Time of the Dreyfus Affair* (Oxford, 1971); Eugene Black, *The Social Politics of Anglo–Jewry, 1880–1920* (Oxford, 1988); Moses Rischin, *The Promised City: New York's Jews, 1870–1914* (Cambridge, MA, and London, 1977), pp. 95–111; Irving Howe, *World of Our Fathers: The Journey of the East European Jews to America and the Life They Found and Made* (New York and London, 1976); Ronald Sanders, *The Downtown Jews: Portraits of an Immigrant Generation* [1969] (New York, 1987); Jonathan Frankel, *Prophecy and Politics: Socialism, Nationalism, and the Russian Jews, 1862–1917* (Cambridge, 1981), pp. 453–551; Lloyd Gartner, *The Jewish Immigrant in England, 1870–1914* (London, 1960); William J. Fishman, *East End Jewish Radicals, 1875–1914* (London, 1975); Michael Meyer with Michael Brenner, eds, *German–Jewish History in Modern Times*, vols 3 and 4 (New York, 1997–8).

16 See *Lewis Hine. Passionate Journey: Photographs 1905–1937*, ed. Karl Steinorth (Rochester, NY, 1996): 'Armenian Jew, Ellis Island Immigrant, New York ca. 1926', p. 40, and 'Street Scene, New York ca. 1910', p. 66; Judith Mara Gutman, *Lewis W. Hine, 1874–1940: Two Perspectives* (New York, 1974): 'Young Russian Jew, Ellis Island, 1905', p. 11, and 'Elderly Jewish Immigrant, Ellis Island, 1905', p. 13. Hine is probably best remembered for his pictures of child labour which were used to reform labour laws; see Russell Freedman, *Kids at Work: Lewis Hine and the Crusade Against Child Labor* (New York, 1994).

17 Paula Hyman, 'Was There a "Jewish Politics" in Western and Central Europe?', in *The Quest for Utopia: Jewish Political Ideas and Institutions Through the Ages*, ed. Zvi Gitelman (Armonk, NY, 1992), pp. 105–17.

18 In contrast to the theoretical literature on the public sphere and 'picture theory', ethnographic research and theory, and 'cultural studies' have integrated Jewish concerns rather well; see Boyarin and Boyarin, *Jews and Other Differences*; Michael M. J. Fischer, 'Ethnicity and the Post-Modern Arts of Memory', in *Writing Culture: The Poetics and Politics of Ethnography*, ed. James Clifford and George E. Marcus (Berkeley, 1986), pp. 194–233; Jack Kugelmass, *The Miracle of Intervale Avenue: The Story of a Jewish Congregation in the South Bronx* (New York, 1996). The main difference between the current project and such ethnographic work is that, as this is a history, I seek explicitly to explain the Jewish community's transition over time, as opposed to dissecting a particular historical moment.

19 Bill Williams, *The Making of Manchester Jewry, 1740–1875* (New York, 1976), p. viii.

20 See Ranajit Guha and Gayatri Chakroavorty Spivak, eds, *Selected Subaltern Studies* (New York and Oxford, 1988).

21 I am greatly indebted to theoretical discussions of 'reception', 'the pictorial turn', 'the public sphere', and 'spectatorship' for the development of this study. Nevertheless, even extremely useful and wise discussions usually do not take into account an ethnic-national 'other' in a historically grounded fashion. Nor should they be expected to. My main point here is that one should not look for insights about Jews (or Italians, Slovaks, or Poles, for that matter) in the mountain of relevant theoretical literature. The most notable exception is the work of John Tagg.

22 Lawrence W. Levine, 'The Historian and the Icon: Photography and the History of American People in the 1930s and 1940s', in *Modern Art and Society: An Anthology of Social and Multicultural Readings*, ed. Maurice Berger (New York, 1994), pp. 182–3.

23 Anthony D. Smith, *The Ethnic Origins of Nations* (Oxford and Cambridge, MA, 1993), p. 5.

24 See Gunther Kress and Theo van Leeuwen, *Reading Images: The Grammar of Visual Design* (London and New York, 1996), pp. 32–3; see Roland Barthes, 'Rhetoric of the Image', in his *Image–Music–Text*, trans. Stephen Heath (New York, 1977), pp. 36, 42–6.

25 Testimonial of Edward F. McGrath in Ephim H. Jeshurin, *B. C. Vladeck: Fifty Years of Life and Labor* (New York, 1936), pp. 7, 14.

26 Melech Epstein, *Profiles of Eleven: Profiles of Eleven Men Who Guided the Destiny of an Immigrant Society and Stimulated Social Consciousness Among the American People* (Detroit, 1965), p. 298; David H. Weinberg, *Between Tradition and Modernity: Haim Zhitlowski, Simon Dubnow, Ahad Ha-Am, and the Shaping of Modern Jewish Identity* (New York and London, 1996), pp. 83–144; Frankel, *Prophecy and Politics*, pp. 258–87.

27 'Isaac Lieb Peretz', in *Dictionary of Jewish Biography*, ed. Geoffrey Wigoder (New York, 1991), p. 394.

28 Marc Bloch, *The Historian's Craft*, trans. Peter Putnam (New York, 1953), pp. 64–5, 80, 130.

29 Laurence Silberstein, 'Cultural Criticism, Ideology, and the Interpretation of Zionism: Toward a Post-Zionist Discourse', in *Interpreting Judaism in a Postmodern Age*, ed. Steven Kepnes (New York, 1996), pp. 325–58.

30 See Martin Jay, 'Vision in Context: Reflections and Refractions', in *Vision in Context: Historical and Contemporary Perspectives on Sight*, ed. Teresa Brennan and Martin Jay (New York and London, 1996), p. 3.

31 Teresa Brennan, '"The Contexts of Vision" from a Specific Standpoint', in *Vision in Context*, ed. Brennan and Jay, p. 219.

32 See Tamar Manor-Friedman, ed., *Workers and Revolutionaries: The Jewish Labor Movement* (Tel Aviv, 1994).

33 Richard Cohen, *Jewish Icons*; John Efron, *Defenders of the Race: Jewish Doctors and Race Science in Fin-de-Siècle Europe* (New Haven, 1994); James E. Young, *The Texture of Memory: Holocaust Memorials and Meaning* (New Haven, 1993); Sander L. Gilman, *Franz Kafka: The Jewish Patient* (New York, 1995).

34 Political cartoons will not be considered here, as they deserve to be treated as a separate genre; see Frankel, *Prophecy and Politics*, pp. 453–551 and Manor-Friedman, *Workers and Revolutionaries*.

35 Levine, 'The Historian and the Icon', p. 194.

36 See W.J.T. Mitchell, *Picture Theory: Essays on Verbal and Visual Representation* (Chicago, 1984), p. 420.

37 This may be compared to images in advertising which are obviously make-
    believe. The main exception will be pictured biblical heroes, which occurred
    most often in literature for children, such as the covers of *Kinder Tshurnal*.

38 See Susan Buck-Morss, *The Dialectics of Seeing: Walter Benjamin and the
    Arcades Project* (Cambridge, MA, and London, 1989), pp. 92–3.

39 To a certain extent, this was even true of Jewish silent films, despite the impor-
    tance of commercialism; see Miriam Hansen, *Babel in Babylon: Spectatorship in
    American Silent Film* (Cambridge, MA, and London, 1991), p. 71.

40 Rosalie Gassman-Sherr, *The Story of The Federation of Women Zionists of Great
    Britain and Ireland, 1918–1968* (London, 1968), p. 8.

41 Testimonials of Daniel W. Hoan and David Dubinsky in Jeshurin, *B. C. Vladeck*,
    pp. 7, 14.

42 'In Memoriam', in *Gewerkschaften: Jubilee Book*, ed. Harry Lang and Morris
    Feinstone (New York, 1938), p. 62.

43 Benedict Anderson, *Imagined Communities: Reflections on the Origin and Spread
    of Nationalism* (London, 1983).

44 See A. L. Epstein, *Ethos and Identity* (London, 1978); Smith, *Ethnic Origins of
    Nations*, p. 14.

45 Roland Barthes, 'The Photographic Message', in his *Image–Music–Text*, p. 15.

46 See Smith, *Ethnic Origins of Nations*, p. 15; 'Ethnicism is fundamentally defen-
    sive. It is a response to outside threats and divisions within . . . It emerges when
    the group's sense of ethnicity is attenuated and impaired, or when it is chal-
    lenged by shattering external events' (*Ibid.*, p. 55).

47 Jurgen Habermas, *The Structural Transformation of the Public Sphere*, trans.
    Thomas Burger and Fredrick Lawrence (Cambridge, MA, 1989), p. 27, quoted
    in Mitchell, *Picture Theory*, p. 363.

48 Benjamin, 'The Work of Art'.

49 Hansen, *Babel and Babylon*, pp. 12–13, 92, 110.

50 See Ritchie Robertson, *Heine* (New York, 1988), p. 61; Walter Benjamin, *Charles
    Baudelaire: A Lyric Poet in the Age of High Capitalism*, trans. Harry Zohn and
    Quentin Hoare (London, 1973); Albrecht Betz, 'Commodity and Modernity in
    Heine and Benjamin', *New German Critique*, 33 (Fall 1984), pp. 179–88.

51 See Mitchell, *Picture Theory*, pp. 11–34.

52 Steinberg, 'Introduction', in Steinberg, *Walter Benjamin and the Demands of
    History*, p. 3.

53 See the debates over divergent readings of Panofsky in Mitchell, *Picture Theory*,
    pp. 13, 16–19, 22–34; and Michael Ann Holly, *Panofsky and the Foundations of
    Art History* (Ithaca, 1984).

54 Holly, *Panofsky*, pp. 14–15.

55 Peter Schmidt, *Aby M. Warburg und die Ikonologie* (Bamberg, 1989); Werner
    Hofmann, Georg Syamken, and Martin Warnke, *Die Menschenrechte des Auges:
    Über Aby Warburg* (Frankfurt a.M., 1980); E. H. Gombrich, *Aby Warburg: An
    Intellectual Biography* (Oxford, 1986).

56 Steinberg, 'Aby Warburg's Kruezlingen Lecture', pp. 82–7.

57 Steinberg, 'Introduction', p. 3.

58 Walter Benjamin, 'Theses on the Philosophy of History', in *Illuminations*, ed.
    Arendt, p. 263.

59 See Peter Novick, *That Noble Dream: The 'Objectivity Question' and the
    American Historical Profession* (Cambridge, 1993), pp. 25–31, on the use and
    abuse of Ranke's legacy, particularly among American historians.

60 Benjamin, 'Theses on the Philosophy of History', p. 264.

61 Gershom Scholem, *From Berlin to Jerusalem: Memories of My Youth*, trans.

Harry Zohn (New York, 1980), p. 28; David Biale, *Gershom Scholem: Kabbalah and Counter-History* (Cambridge, MA, 1979), p. 53.

62 'Die Congress-Medaille', *Die Welt*, 5 August 1898, p. 5.

63 *Handbook of Trade Union Methods with Special Reference to the Garment Trades* (New York, 1937), p. 54.

64 *Ibid.*

65 John A. Dyche, *Bolshevism in American Labor Unions: A Plea for Constructive Unionism* (New York, 1926).

66 Wiley Britton, *The White Slavery: A Study of the Present Trade Union System* (Akron, OH, 1909).

67 Hansen, *Babel and Babylon*, p. 92.

68 David Biale, *Power and Powerlessness in Jewish History* (New York, 1987).

69 See Hansen, *Babel and Babylon*, p. 71.

70 Levine, 'The Historian and the Icon', p. 173.

71 Hansen, *Babel and Babylon*, p. 74.

72 Benzion Eisenstadt, *Hakhme Yisrael ba-Amerika* (New York, 1903).

73 See Kugelmass, 'Jewish Icons', p. 33.

74 *Jüdischer Almanach 5670: Bar-Kochba in Wien* (Cologne, 1910).

75 'Jüdische Kriegspostkarten', produced by the Lamm Verlag, Berlin 1915; see Steinberg, 'Aby Warburg's Kruezlingen Lecture', pp. 82–7.

76 Arnold Zweig and Hermann Struck, *Das ostjüdische Antlitz* [1920] (Wiesbaden, 1988).

77 Jacob Magidoff, *Des shpigel fun der ist sayd* (New York, 1923); this is the source of a number of portraits by Saul Raskin, for which copyright is held by the American Jewish Archives.

78 Yaakov Benor-Kalter, *Photographs of the New Working Palestine* (Haifa, 1935).

79 Tagg, *Burden of Representation*, p. 16.

80 A popular expression is found in the conclusion of John Berger, *Ways of Seeing* (London, 1987): 'Publicity is the life of this culture – in so far as without publicity capitalism could not survive – and at the same time publicity is its dream . . . Capitalism survives by forcing the majority, whom it exploits, to define their own interests as narrowly as possible. This was once achieved by extensive deprivation. Today in the developed countries it is being achieved by imposing a false standard of what is and what is not desirable' (p. 154).

81 See Oskar Negt and Alexander Kluge, *Public Sphere and Experience: Toward an Analysis of the Bourgeois and Proletarian Public Sphere*, foreword by Miriam Hansen, trans. Peter Labanyi, Jamie Owen Daniel, and Assenka Oksiloff (Minneapolis and London, 1993).

82 Nathaniel Spector, in *Gewerkschaften: Jubilee Book*, ed. Lang and Feinstone, pp. 83–4.

83 See Roger Chartier, 'Texts, Printing, Reading', in *The New Cultural History*, ed. Lynn Hunt (Berkeley, 1989), p. 169.

84 Rose Schneiderman with Lucy Goldthwaite, *All for One* (New York, 1967), p. 108.

85 See Negt and Kluge, *Public Sphere and Experience*, p. 39.

86 Vernon L. Lidtke, *The Alternative Culture: Socialist Labor in Imperial Germany* (New York, 1985).

87 See Stephen Koch, *Stalin, Willi Muenzenberg and the Seduction of the Intellectuals* (London, 1995), for the 'revised' account of Muenzenberg's career.

88 Quoted in Halla Beloff, *Camera Culture* (New York, 1985), pp. 129–30.

89 Melech Epstein, *Pages from a Colorful Life: An Autobiographical Sketch* (Miami Beach, 1971), p. 17.

90 Melech Epstein, *Profiles of Eleven*, p. 19.

91 Contained in the 'Yiddish Song Database' of the Robert and Molly Freedman Archive of Jewish Music at the University of Pennsylvania, Philadelphia, Pennsylvania.

92 See Levine, 'The Historian and the Icon', p. 194.

93 Peter Paret, *Art as History: Episodes in the Culture and Politics of Nineteenth-Century Germany* (Princeton, 1988), p. 9.

94 Mitchell, *Picture Theory*, p.5.

95 See Richard Leppert, *Art and the Committed Eye: The Cultural Functions of Imagery* (Boulder, 1995), p. 3.

96 Tagg, *Burden of Representation*, p. 2.

97 Levine, 'The Historian and the Icon', p. 173.

98 *Ibid.*, p. 184.

99 Leppert, *Art and the Committed Eye*, p. 10.

100 Alan Sekula, *Photography Against the Grain: Essays and Photo Works, 1973–1983* (Halifax, 1984), p. 7, quoted in Levine, 'The Historian and the Icon', p. 173.

101 Leppert, *Art and the Committed Eye*, p. 6; see also Mitchell, *Picture Theory*, p. 324.

102 Jay, 'Vision in Context', p. 7.

103 See David Freedberg, *The Power of Images: Studies in the History and Theory of Response* (Chicago and London, 1991), p. 440.

104 Hansen, *Babel and Babylon*, p. 1.

105 *Die Welt*, 3 September 1897, p. 12.

106 Irma Lindheim, *The Immortal Adventure* (New York, 1928), pp. 22–3.

107 Michael Berkowitz, *Zionist Culture and West European Jewry Before the First World War* (Cambridge, 1993), pp. 28–30, 136–8.

108 Edward King, *Joseph Zalmonah* (Boston, 1893), pp. 11, 32, 260, 335.

109 *Ibid.*, p. 244.

110 Melech Epstein, *Profiles of Eleven*, p. 115.

111 Schneiderman with Goldthwaite, *All for One*, pp. 241–2.

112 Gassman-Sherr, *Story of the Federation*, pp. 8–9.

113 Arthur Hertzberg, ed., *The Zionist Idea: A Historical Analysis and Reader* [1959] (New York, 1986); Shlomo Avineri, *The Making of Modern Zionism: The Intellectual Origins of the Jewish State* (New York, 1981).

114 Melech Epstein, *Profiles of Eleven*; Magidoff, *Des shpigel*.

115 Jonathan Sarna, *JPS: The Americanization of Jewish Culture, 1888–1988* (Philadelphia, 1989), pp. 47–94.

116 Howe, *World of Our Fathers*, p. 90.

117 See Joan Wallach Scott, *Gender and the Politics of History* (New York, 1988), pp. 25–6.

118 On Zionism, see Michael Berkowitz, *Western Jewry and the Zionist Project, 1914–1933* (Cambridge, 1997).

119 On the myth of Trumpeldor in the context of the Yishuv, see Yael Zerubavel, *Recovered Roots: Collective Memory and the Making of the Israeli National Tradition* (Chicago, 1995); see Michael Brown, *The Israeli–American Connection: Its Roots in the Yishuv, 1914–1945* (Detroit, 1997), pp. 35–68.

120 Hapgood, *Spirit of the Ghetto*, p. 235.

121 *Ibid.*, p. 232.

122 *Ibid.*, pp. 192–3.

123 *Ibid.*, p. 198.

124 *Ibid.*, p. 196.

125 Y. S. Hertz, *Fuftzig yor arbeter-ring in yidishn lebn* (New York, 1950); see pictures

of Arbeter Ring cemetery in New York and the Arbeter Ring sanitorium in Liberty, NY; Maximillian Hurwitz, *The Workman's Circle: Its History, Ideals, Organization and Institutions* (New York, 1936), pp. 108–9; Morris C. Feinstone, 'A Brief History of the United Hebrew Trades', in *Gewerkschaften: Jubilee Book*, ed. Lang and Feinstone, p. 27.

126 Lionel Kochan, *Beyond the Graven Image: A Jewish View* (London, 1997).

127 See Nathan Birnbaum, *Im Dienste der Verheissung* (Frankfurt a.M., 1927); Joshua A. Fishman, *Ideology, Society, and Language: The Odyssey of Nathan Birnbaum* (Ann Arbor, 1987).

128 See Richard Cohen, *Jewish Icons*, pp. 151–3.

129 See Stuart A. Cohen, *English Zionists and British Jews: The Communal Politics of Anglo–Jewry, 1895–1920* (Princeton, 1982), pp. 112–13.

130 Hurwitz, *The Workmen's Circle*, p. 108.

131 Entry for 13 July 1896, in *The Diaries of Theodor Herzl*, ed. Marvin Lowenthal (Gloucester, MA, 1978), p. 180.

132 Isidore Nagler, 'The Jewish Trade Unions and the Gewerkschaften', in *Gewerkschaften: Jubilee Book*, ed. Lang and Feinstone, p. 59. On 'vicarious' nationalism in general, see Smith, *Ethnic Origins of Nations*, p. 152; on Zionism, see Michael Berkowitz, *Zionist Culture* and *Western Jewry and the Zionist Project*, and Ezra Mendelsohn, *On Modern Jewish Politics* (New York, 1993).

133 Joseph Leftwich, introduction to Rudolf Rocker, *The London Years*, trans. Joseph Leftwich (London, 1956), p. 31.

134 Harry Lang and Morris Feinstone, eds, *Gewerkschaften* (New York, 1928), p. 31.

135 Feinstone, 'Brief History', p. 24.

136 See Daniel Soyer, *Jewish Immigrant Associations and American Identity in New York, 1880–1939* (London and Cambridge, MA, 1997).

137 King, *Zalmonah*, p. 83.

138 Carl Degler, *Out of Our Past: The Forces that Shaped Modern America*, rev. edn (New York, 1970), p. 265.

139 Eli Lederhendler, *The Road to Modern Jewish Politics: Political Tradition and Political Reconstruction in the Jewish Community of Tsarist Russia* (New York, 1989).

140 Warren Sussman, *Culture as History: The Transformation of American Society in the Twentieth Century* (New York, 1984), p. 160, quoted in Levine, 'The Historian and the Icon', p. 197.

141 Beloff, *Camera Culture*, p. 22, quoted in Kugelmass, 'Jewish Icons', p. 30.

142 Benjamin, 'Theses on the Philosophy of History', p. 264.

2 *The Gallery of Zionists*

1 Carl E. Schorske, *Fin-de-Siècle Vienna: Politics and Culture* (New York, 1981), pp. 146–74; Robert Wistrich, *The Jews of Vienna in the Age of Franz Josef* (Oxford, 1990), pp. 421–93; Amos Elon, *Herzl* (New York, 1975); Ernst Pawel, *The Labyrinth of Exile: A Life of Theodor Herzl* (New York, 1989).

2 Theodor Herzl, diary entries for 15 July 1896 and 3 September 1897, in *The Diaries of Theodor Herzl*, ed. Marvin Lowenthal (Gloucester, MA, 1978), pp. 182–3, 224–5.

3 Theodor Herzl, 'Opening Address at the Second Zionist Congress' (delivered in Basel on 28 August 1898), in Herzl, *Zionist Writings, vol. II: Essays and Addresses*, trans. Harry Zohn (New York, 1975), pp. 16–17.

4 See Michael Brown, *The Israeli–American Connection: Its Roots in the Yishuv, 1914–1945* (Detroit, 1997), pp. 212–13, 186–8, 92–3.

5 Quoted in Pawel, *Labyrinth of Exile*, p. 456; Pawel, in this translation, mistook the name 'Neuda' for Nordau.

6 Robert S. Wistrich, 'Theodor Herzl: The Making of a Political Messiah', in *The Shaping of Israeli Identity: Myth, Memory, and Trauma*, ed. Robert Wistrich and David Ohana (London and Portland, OR, 1995), pp. 1–37.

7 Ben-Ami, quoted in Alex Bein, *Theodore Herzl: A Biography* (Philadelphia, 1943), pp. 231–2.

8 Jacob De Haas, *Theodor Herzl: A Biographical Study*, 2 vols. (Chicago and New York, 1927), vol.II; there is no mention in the text of the portrait.

9 Hermann Struck, reproduction of etching of Theodor Herzl, in *Jüdischer Almanach II*, ed. Berthold Fiewel (Berlin, 1904), p. 107.

10 Teachers of the Jerusalem Hebrew Gymnasium, 2286, photo collection, CZA.

11 David Tartakover, ed., *Herzl in Profile: Herzl's Image in the Applied Arts* (Tel Aviv, 1979), pp. 28, 30, 19, 27.

12 See Arnold Zweig and Hermann Struck, *Das ostjüdische Antlitz* (Wiesbaden, 1988); originally published in 1920, with 25 pictures by Hermann Struck. See also David Brenner, *Marketing Identities: The Invention of Jewish Ethnicity in Ost und West* (Detroit, 1998); Noah Isenberg, *Between Redemption and Doom: The Strains of German–Jewish Modernism* (Lincoln, NE, 1999).

13 Arnold Fortlage and Karl Schwarz, *Das graphische Werk von Hermann Struck* (Berlin, 1911), pp. 1–3; Heinrich Hirschberg, *Der Humor bei Struck* (Berlin, 1919); Adolph Donath, *Hermann Struck* (Berlin, 1920).

14 Israel Zangwill, introduction to a portfolio of heliogravures by E. M. Lilien, *The Holy Land* (Berlin and Vienna, 1922), no pagination.

15 See Michael Berkowitz, *Zionist Culture and West European Jewry Before the First World War* (Cambridge, 1993), pp. 127–9.

16 Richard Cohen, *Jewish Icons: Art and Society in Modern Europe* (Berkeley, 1998), pp. 241–4.

17 'Moses zebricht die Tafeln', in *Die Bücher der Bibel* (Berlin, 1908), p. 51; David Tartakover, *Herzl in Profile: Herzl's Image in the Applied Arts* (Tel Aviv, 1979), p. 7.

18 One of these spelled his name, uncharacteristically, as 'Theodore Hertzl'.

19 See Richard Cohen, *Jewish Icons*, p. 266, n. 25; Elliot Horowitz, 'Visages du judaism: de la barbe en monde juif et de l'élaboration de ses significations', *Annales Histoire, Sciences Sociales*, 49 (1994), pp. 1080–6.

20 *Jewish Chronicle*, 12 September 1913, pp. 18, 26; *Jewish Chronicle*, 18 August 1911, p. 22.

21 Reproduction of portrait of Isaac Hourwich in AJA; Melech Epstein, *Profiles of Eleven: Profiles of Eleven Men Who Guided The Destiny of an Immigrant Society and Stimulated Social Consciousness Among the American People* (Detroit, 1965), p. 267.

22 Melech Epstein, *Profiles of Eleven*, p. 138.

23 Lionel S. Reiss, 'Through Artists' Eyes: The Portraits of Herzl as Revelations of the Man', in Meyer Weisgel, ed., *Theodor Herzl: A Memorial* (New York, 1929), pp. 113–14.

24 Bessie Thomashevsky, *Mayn lebns-geshikhte* (New York, 1916), pp. 198–9; S. Niger, *Dertseylers un romanistn* (New York, 1946), vol. 1, p. 198; quoted in Joel Berkowitz, 'Shakespeare on the American Yiddish Stage', PhD dissertation, City University of New York, 1995, pp. 51–3.

25 Joel Berkowitz, 'Shakespeare in Yiddish', p. 51.

26 See Neal Gabler, *An Empire of Their Own: How the Jews Invented Hollywood* (New York, 1989).

27 See Michael Berkowitz, *Zionist Culture*, pp. 43–5.

28 George L. Mosse, *Nationalism and Sexuality: Respectability and Abnormal Sexuality in Modern Europe* (New York, 1985), pp. 66–89.

29 Morris Hillquit, *Loose Leaves from a Busy Life* (New York, 1934).

30 Wistrich, *Jews of Vienna*, pp. 347–80; Erwin Rosenberger, *Herzl as I Remember Him*, trans. Louis Jay Hermann (New York, 1959).

31 M. Amit, *ha-Meri: perakim mi-ma'avak ha-kiyum shel ha-Yahadut ha-haredit be-erets-Yisrael* [The Uprising: Chapters from the Struggle for Existence of Haredi Jewry in the Land of Israel] (Bene Beraq, [*c.* 1982]).

32 Postcard with Herzl surrounded by Nordau, Moses Gaster, Bernard Lazare, and Mandelstamm, ZP15.903, photo collection, CZA.

33 Stephen Wise, *Challenging Years: The Autobiography of Steven Wise* (New York, 1949), p. 29.

34 Max Nordau, 'II. Kongressrede (Basel, 28. August 1898)', in *Max Nordaus zionistische Schriften* (Cologne and Leipzig, 1909), p. 64.

35 See Nelly Wilson, *Bernard Lazare: Antisemitism and the Problem of Jewish Identity in Late Nineteenth-Century France* (Cambridge, 1978).

36 Herzl to Ahad Ha-Am, 24 July 1897, HNIII 368, HB 751, CZA.

37 Ahad Ha-Am, 'The First Zionist Congress', trans. S. Weinstein, in *The Jew in the Modern World: A Documentary History*, 2nd edn, ed. Jehuda Reinharz and Paul Mendes-Flohr (New York, 1995), p. 543.

38 David Vital, *Zionism: The Formative Years* (Oxford, 1982), p. 15

39 See 'Prof. Max Mandelstamm' in Max Raisin, *A History of the Jews in Modern Times*, 5th edn (New York, 1937), p. 423; Herzl file, CZA.

40 Theodor Herzl, diary entry for 13 July 1896, in *Diaries of Herzl*, ed. Lowenthal, p. 180.

41 Maximillian Hurwitz, *The Workman's Circle: Its History, Ideals, Organization and Institutions* (New York, 1936), p. 108.

42 Herbert H. Lehman to Morris C. Feinstone, in *Gewerkschaften: Jubilee Book*, ed. Harry Lang and Morris Feinstone (New York, 1938), p. 66.

43 *Der Hamer* (November 1930), p. 46.

44 Annelise Orleck, *Common Sense and a Little Fire: Women and Working-Class Politics in the United States, 1900–1965* (Chapel Hill and London, 1995).

45 In the few instances when he did speak out on Jewish topics, Nordau was less than sympathetic to traditional views of Judaism, and this was used against him in the controversy over Herzl's utopian novel, *Altneuland* (Leipzig, 1902); see 'Die Juden von Gestern' (Eine Erwiderung), *Ost und West*, 4 (April 1903), pp. 225–6.

46 Milton P. Foster, 'The Reception of Max Nordau's "Degeneration" in England and America', PhD dissertation, University of Michigan, 1954, pp. 2, 40; *Jewish Chronicle*, 9 February 1923, p. 10; *Palestine Weekly* (Jerusalem), 26 January 1923, p. 53; the latter points out that this was sometimes due to anti-Semitism.

47 Israel Zangwill, 'Nordau and Abarbanel' (1923), in *Speeches, Articles, and Letters of Israel Zangwill*, ed. Maurice Simon (London, 1937), p. 146; Meir Ben-Horin, *Max Nordau: Philosopher of Human Solidarity* (London, 1956).

48 'Max Nordau at work. Drawing by Maxa Nordau', frontispiece, and cover portrait, in Anna Nordau and Maxa Nordau, *Max Nordau: A Biography* (New York, 1943).

49 In De Haas, *Herzl*, vol. II, opp. p. 32.

50 *Stenographisches Protokoll der Verhandlungen des VIII. Zionisten-Kongress in Haag vom 14. bis inklusive 21. August 1907* (Cologne, 1907), pp. 53ff., 255ff.

51 See Marjorie Lamberti, 'Jewish Defense in Germany after the Nazi Seizure of

Power', *Year Book of the Leo Baeck Institute*, XLII (1997), pp. 135–47.

52 Compare Brown, *Israeli–American Connection*.

53 Max Nordau, 'Was bedeutet Turnen für uns Juden?', *Jüdische Turnzeitung* (July 1902), pp. 109–12.

54 Gershom Scholem, *From Berlin to Jerusalem: Memories of My Youth*, trans. Harry Zohn (New York, 1980), p. 23.

55 See Paul Breines, *Tough Jews: Political Fantasies and the Moral Dilemma of American Jewry* (New York, 1990).

56 Eddie Cantor, 'Foreword', to Barney Ross and Martin Abramson, *No Man Stands Alone* (London, 1959), pp. 11, 14, 19.

57 James Huntington-Whiteley, *The Book of British Sporting Heroes* (London, 1998), p. 152; Morton Lewis, *Ted Kid Lewis: His Life and Times* (London, 1990).

58 John Harding with Jack 'Kid' Berg, *Jack Kid Berg: The Whitechapel Windmill* (London, 1987).

59 *Ibid.*, p. 162.

60 *Ibid.*, pp. 103–4.

61 *Weizmann der Führer: Anlässlich seines Besuches in Brünn im Januar 1925* (Prague [?], 1925), p. 8; Israel Cohen, 'Weizmanns Aufstieg: sein Verhältnis zu dem Staatsmännern Englands', in *Weizmann der Führer*, pp. 11–15.

62 *Weizmann der Führer*, pp. 5, 3.

63 'Editorial Comments: Dropping the Pilot', *Pioneer* (July 1931), p. 3.

64 *Weizmann der Führer*, pp. 6ff.

65 A. D. Lineator, in *Monthly Pioneer* (August 1928), p. 8.

66 S. M. Melamed, 'Chaim Weizmann: Man and Zionist', *Maccabaean*, December 1917, p. 427..

67 Chaim Weizmann, 'Lay Down Your Arms', *New Maccabaean*, 20 May 1921, pp. 23–4.

68 'Chajim Weizmann: zum 50. Geburtstag (27. November 1923)', *Jüdische Rundschau*, 27 November 1923, p. 575.

69 See Chaim Weizmann to Theodor Herzl, May 6, 1903, in *The Letters and Papers of Chaim Weizmann*, II, gen. ed. Meyer Weisgal (London, 1971), pp. 312–13.

70 'American Zionists Welcome Dr. Weizmann. Reception in New York City Marks First Public Appearance Since Arrival Here as President of the World Zionist Organization: Louis Lipsky Scorns Zionist Detractors', *New Palestine*, 6 April 1928, p. 402.

71 Irma Lindheim, *The Immortal Adventure* (New York, 1928), pp. 22–3.

72 Bernard Richards, 'Louis Brandeis', *Jüdische Rundschau*, 20 November 1914, p. 437.

73 On Brandeis's early career, see Allon Gal, *Brandeis of Boston* (Cambridge, MA, 1980); Gal, 'Brandeis, Judaism, and Zionism', in *Brandeis and America*, ed. Nelson L. Dawson (Lexington, KY, 1989), pp. 65–98; Philippa Strum, *Brandeis: Beyond Progressivism* (Lawrence, KS, 1993); Strum, *Louis D. Brandeis: Justice of the People* (Cambridge, MA, 1984).

74 I. J. Klingler, 'Louis D. Brandeis', *Yedioth Hadassah* (October–November 1941); translated excepts in Brandeis file, Box 2, Folder 1, Hadassah Archives.

75 L.L. [Louis Lipsky], 'Mr. Justice Brandeis', *Maccabaean* (November 1916), p. 79; De Haas, *Herzl*.

76 'Brandeis in Leadership', editorial in *Der Tog*, 14 August 1930; translated English typescript in A 406/94, CZA.

77 Jacob De Haas, 'Louis Dembitz Brandeis – Zionist', *Jewish Tribune*, 12 November 1926, p. 5.

78 Jessie Sampter, 'A New Leader', *Young Judaean* (December 1914), pp. 4, 12.

79 Mrs Sol Rosenbloom, in *Jewish Tribune*, 12 November 1926, p. 4.

80 Address delivered by Henrietta Szold at the Brandeis Memorial Meeting, Ein Hashophet, 16 October 1941, Brandeis file, Box 1, Folder 9, Hadassah Archives.

81 Compare Aaron Berman, *Nazism, the Jews, and American Zionism, 1933–1948* (Detroit, 1990), p. 18; see Michael Berkowitz, *Western Jewry and the Zionist Project, 1914–1933* (Cambridge, 1997).

82 Wise, *Challenging Years*, p. 23.

83 *Ibid.*, pp. 204, 315.

84 David S. Wyman, *The Abandonment of the Jews: America and the Holocaust, 1941–1945* (New York, 1985), p. 69.

85 *Ibid.*

86 Quoted in Moses Rischin, *The Promised City: New York's Jews, 1870–1914* (Cambridge, MA, and London, 1977), pp. 247–8.

87 Mrs Edward Jacobs, in Brandeis Memorial Session, 27th Annual Convention of Hadassah, Hotel William Penn, Pittsburgh, 2 November 1941, pp. 4–11; Box 1, Folder 9, Hadassah Archives.

88 See Donald H. Miller, 'A History of Hadassah 1912–1935', PhD dissertation, New York University, 1968; Carol Bosworth Kutscher, 'The Early Years of Hadassah, 1912–1921', PhD dissertation, Brandeis University, 1976; Joan Dash, *Summoned to Jerusalem: The Life of Henrietta Szold* (New York, 1979); Irving Fineman, *Woman of Valor* (New York, 1961); Rose Zeitlin, *Henrietta Szold* (New York, 1952); Elma Levinger, *Fighting Angel* (New York, 1946); Szold, *Henrietta Szold: Life and Letters*, ed. Marvin Lowenthal (New York, 1942); Irma Lindheim, *Parallel Quest: A Search of a Person and a People* (New York, 1962). For the larger theoretical frameworks for investigating the role of women in Zionism, see Claudia Prestel, 'Frauen und die Zionistische Bewegung (1897–1933): Tradition oder Revolution?', *Historische Zeitschrift*, 258 (1994), pp. 29–71.

89 'Men and Matters', *Monthly Pioneer* (March 1929), p. 9.

90 Morris C. Feinstone, 'A Brief History of the United Hebrew Trades', in *Gewerkschaften: Jubilee Book*, ed. Lang and Feinstone, p. 24.

91 Arthur Hertzberg, ed., *The Zionist Idea: A Historical Analysis and Reader* (New York, 1986); Shlomo Avineri, *The Making of Modern Zionism: Intellectual Origins of the Jewish State* (New York, 1981).

92 On the reception of Einstein, from a cultural perspective, see Alan J. Friedman and Carol C. Donley, *Einstein as Myth and Muse* (Cambridge, 1989); Gerald Holton and Yehuda Elkana, eds, *Albert Einstein: Historical and Cultural Perspectives* (Princeton, 1982), pp. 281–343.

93 Nahum Goldmann, *Mein Leben als deutscher Jude* (Munich, 1980), pp. 177–8.

94 Herman Bernstein, *Celebrities of Our Time* (London, 1924), p. 243.

95 Stephen S. Wise to Julian Mack, 17 December 1930, MSS Col. 19, 25/15, AJA.

96 Portrait of Einstein by Max Liebermann on cover of *Menorah* (Paris Zionist organ), 1 April 1928.

97 *Jüdische Rundschau*, 24 June 1921, p. 359; 'Der Aufbau Palästinas als Aufgabe der Judenheit: eine jüdische Massenkundgebung in Berlin', *Jüdische Rundschau*, 6 July 1921, p. 371.

98 'Professor Einstein über sein Eindrücke in Palästina', *Jüdische Rundschau*, 24 April 1923, pp. 195–6; 'Eine Botschschaft Einsteins: die Antwort auf das Weissbuch muss verdoppelte Arbeit sein', *Jüdische Rundschau*, 5 December 1930, p. 644.

99 See 'Das Echo des Einstein-Briefes', *Jüdische Rundschau*, 22 October 1929, p. 555, on the impact of Einstein's letter to the *Manchester Guardian* of 12

October 1929.

100 'Prof. Einstein fährt nach Palästina', *Jüdische Rundschau*, 6 October 1922, p. 521; 'Einstein in Singapore', *Jüdische Rundschau*, 5 January 1923, p. 5; 'Einstein in Wien', *Jüdische Rundschau*, 26 September 1924, p. 551; 'Einstein in New York', *Jüdische Rundschau*, 19 December 1930, p. 672.

101 'Einstein in Palästina', *Jüdische Rundschau*, 16 February 1923, p. 75.

102 Yitzhak Navon, 'On Einstein and the Presidency of Israel', in *Albert Einstein: Historical and Cultural Perspectives*, ed. Holton and Elkana, pp. 293–6.

103 Quoted in Jeremy Bernstein, *Einstein* (New York, 1973), p. 214.

104 Goldmann, *Mein Leben als deutscher Jude*, p. 178.

105 See Steven E. Aschheim, *Brothers and Strangers: East European Jews in German and German–Jewish Consciousness* (Madison, WI, 1982), and Jack Wertheimer, *Unwelcome Strangers: East European Jews in Imperial Germany* (New York and Oxford, 1987).

106 Albert Einstein, 'Assimilation and Nationalism' (1) (1920), in Einstein, *About Zionism*, ed. and trans. Leon Simon (London, 1930), pp. 23–4.

107 Abraham Pais, *Subtle is the Lord: The Science and Life of Albert Einstein* (New York, 1982), pp. 317, 315.

108 Einstein, 'Assimilation and Nationalism' (2) (1920), in his *About Zionism*, pp. 27–8.

109 *Ibid.*, p. 28.

110 *Ibid.*, p. 37.

111 'Einstein an die arabische Welt', *Jüdische Rundschau*, 31 January 1930, p. 57.

112 Leon Simon, introduction to Einstein, *About Zionism*, p. 18.

113 Stuart A. Cohen, *English Zionists and British Jews: The Communal Politics of Anglo–Jewry 1895–1920* (Princeton, 1982), p. 218; Howard M. Sachar, *A History of the Jews in America* (New York, 1992), p. 550.

114 Ezra Mendelsohn, *On Modern Jewish Politics* (New York, 1993).

115 See Jaap Meijer, *De Zoon van een Gazzen: het leven van Jacob Israel De Haan, 1881–1924* (Amsterdam, 1967); Ludy Giebels, 'Jacob Israel De Haan in Palestina, I', *Studia Rosenthaliana*, XIV/1 (January 1980), pp. 44–78; Giebels, 'Jacob Israel De Haan in Palestina, II', *Studia Rosenthaliana*, XV/1 (March 1981), pp. 111–42; Giebels, 'Jacob Israel De Haan in Palestina, III', *Studia Rosenthaliana*, XV/2 (August 1981), pp. 188–233; Giebels, ed., *Jacob Israel De Haan: Correspondent in Palestina, 1919–1924*, special issue of *De Engelbewaarder*, 23 (July 1981); Marijke T. C. Stapert-Eggen, 'The Rosenthaliana's Jacob Israel De Haan Archive', in *Bibliotheca Rosenthaliana. Treasures of Jewish Booklore: Marking the 200th Anniversary of the Birth of Leeser Rosenthal, 1794–1994*, ed. Emile G. L. Schrijver and F. J. Hoogewoud (Amsterdam, 1994), p. 99; Emil Marmorstein, *A Martyr's Message: To Commemorate the Fiftieth Anniversary of the Murder of Professor De-Haan* (London, 1975); Shlomoh Nakdimon, *Deh Han: ha-retsah ha-politi ha-rishon be-Erets-Yisrael* [De Haan: The First Political Assassination in Eretz Israel] (Tel Aviv, 1985); Tsevi Meshi-Zahav and Yehudah Meshi-Zahav, *ha-Kadosh. Rabi Ya'akov Yisrael Deh-Haan ha-y.d.: ha-retsah ha-Tsiyoni harishon be-e. Y.* [The Martyr, Rabbi Jacob Israel De Haan: The First Zionist Murder in Eretz Israel] (Jerusalem, 1986).

116 Govaert C.J.J. van den Bergh, *De taal zegt meer dan zij verantwoorden kan* [Language Contains More than One Can Account For] (Nijmegen, 1994).

117 Michael Berkowitz, 'Doubled Trouble: A Call to Investigate the Life and After-Lives of De Vriendt and De Haan', *Jahrbuch für Internationale Germanistik* A, 49 (1999), pp. 111–24.

3 Greater Deviations

1 'Letters and Greetings from Friends', in *Gewerkschaften: Jubilee Book*, ed. Harry Lang and Morris Feinstone (New York, 1938), pp. 66–7.

2 *Der Hamer* (November 1930), pp. 41–3; William J. Fishman, *East End Jewish Radicals 1875–1914* (London, 1975), pp. 97–134; Jonathan Frankel, *Prophecy and Politics: Socialism, Nationalism, and the Russian Jews, 1862–1917* (Cambridge, 1981), pp. 28–48.

3 Paul Avrich, *Anarchist Voices: An Oral History of Anarchists in America* (Princeton, 1988), pp. 483–4, n. 73.

4 Hyman Berman, 'The Cloakmakers' Strike of 1910', in *Essays on Jewish Life and Thought: Presented in Honor of Salo Wittmayer Baron*, ed. Joseph L. Blau *et al.* (New York, 1959), pp. 67–94; Melech Epstein, *Profiles of Eleven: Profiles of Eleven Men Who Guided The Destiny of an Immigrant Society and Stimulated Social Consciousness Among the American People* (Detroit, 1965), pp. 263–4.

5 Michael Abrahamson, in *Gewerkschaften: Jubilee Book*, ed. Lang and Feinstone, p. 82.

6 Rose Schneiderman with Lucy Goldthwaite, *All for One* (New York, 1967), p. 242.

7 *Bol'shaia sovetskaia entsiklopediia* (Moscow, 1930), vol. 19, pp. 831–2.

8 Marion Kaplan, *Between Dignity and Despair: Jewish Life in Nazi Germany* (New York, 1998).

9 See Tom Segev, *The Seventh Million: The Israelis and the Holocaust*, trans. Haim Watzman (New York, 1992); Abraham Edelheit, *The Yishuv in the Shadow of the Holocaust* (Boulder, 1997).

10 Harriet Freidenreich, *Jewish Politics in Vienna, 1918–1938* (Bloomington, 1991); Sean Martin, 'Ambivalent Opposition: Jewish Political Power in Poland, 1926–1928', MA thesis, Ohio State University, 1994.

11 The standard text remains James Joll, *The Anarchists*, 2nd edn (London, 1979); see also Paul Avrich, *Anarchist Portraits* (Princeton, 1990), pp. 176–99; Herman Frank, *Anarkho-sotsialistishe ideyen un bavegungen bay yidn: historishe un teorishe aynfirung* (Paris, 1951).

12 Avrich, *Anarchist Portraits*, p. 176.

13 Morris Hillquit, *History of Socialism in the United States*, 5th edn (New York, 1971), p. 221.

14 Paul Avrich, 'Rudolf Rocker', in *Rudolf Rocker: A Memorial*, special issue of *The Dandelion*, IV/14 (Summer 1980), pp. 3–4.

15 Mina Graur, *An Anarchist 'Rabbi': The Life and Teachings of Rudolf Rocker* (New York and Jerusalem, 1997).

16 Anne J. Kershen, *Uniting the Tailors: Trade Unionism Amongst the Tailoring Workers of London and Leeds, 1870–1939* (London, 1995), p. 156.

17 Abe Bluestein, 'Memories of Rudolf Rocker', in *Rudolf Rocker: A Memorial*, p. 5.

18 *Ibid.*, p. 7.

19 Max Nordau, *Okonomisher lign* (chapter in Nordau's *Conventional Lies of Our Civilization*), trans. Rudolf Rocker (London, 1904); this was produced as a pamphlet which appropriated floral and agricultural images common to Zionism; 'Rocker, Rudolf (1873–1958)', *Encyclopedia Judaica*.

20 Avrich, *Anarchist Portraits*, p. 178.

21 N. Goldberg, in E. Tscherikower, ed., *Geshikhte fun der yidisher arbeter-bavegung in de fareynikte shtatn*, II (New York, 1945), pp. 297–304.

22 Emma Goldman, *Anarchism and Other Essays* [1917] (New York, 1969), p. 41.

23 Alexander Berkman, forward to Rudolf Rocker, *Johann Most: das Leben eines*

Rebellen (Berlin, 1924), p. 6; Hermia Oliver, *The International Anarchist Movement in Late Victorian London* (London, 1983), pp. 17–19.

24 Avrich, *Anarchist Portraits*, p. 178.

25 Abraham Cahan, 'Johann Most in Court' (16 September 1901), and 'We Find the Defendant Guilty' (12 October 1901), in *Grandma Never Lived in America: The New Journalism of Abraham Cahan*, ed. Moses Rischin (Bloomington, 1985), pp. 342–6.

26 Compare Irving Howe, *World of Our Fathers: The Journey of the East European Jews to America and the Life They Found and Made* (New York and London, 1976), p. 104; Ronald Sanders, *The Downtown Jews: Portraits of an Immigrant Generation* (New York, 1987), pp. 78–9.

27 Hillquit, *Socialism in the United States*, pp. 212–21.

28 Goldberg in Tscherikower, *Geshikhte*, II, p. 302.

29 See Lawrence Baron, 'Erich Muehsam's Jewish Identity', *Year Book of the Leo Baeck Institute*, XXV (1980), pp. 269, 279.

30 Michael Loewy, *Redemption and Utopia. Jewish Libertarian Thought in Central Europe: A Study in Elective Affinity*, trans. Hope Heaney (Stanford, 1992), p. 128.

31 Paul Breines, 'Germans, Journals, and Jews/Madison, Men, Marxism, and Mosse: A Tale of Jewish–Leftist Confusion in America', in *Germans and Jews Since the Holocaust*, ed. Anson Rabinbach and Jack Zipes (New York, 1986), pp. 146–70.

32 Melech Epstein, *Pages from a Colorful Life: An Autobiographical Sketch* (Miami Beach, 1971), pp. 17–18.

33 Ezra Mendelsohn, *Class Struggle in the Pale: The Formative Years of the Jewish Workers' Movement in Tsarist Russia* (Cambridge, 1970).

34 Melech Epstein, *Pages from a Colorful Life*, pp. 17–18.

35 Lloyd P. Gartner, 'Jewish Immigrants in London in the 1880s', in Blau *et al.*, *Essays on Jewish Life and Thought*, p. 245; David Cesarani, *The Jewish Chronicle and Anglo–Jewry, 1841–1991* (Cambridge, 1994), p. 109.

36 Steven Cassedy, *To the Other Shore: The Russian Jewish Intellectuals Who Came to America* (Princeton, 1997), p. 78.

37 *Ibid.*, pp. 119–22.

38 Hutchins Hapgood, *The Spirit of the Ghetto* [1902], ed. Moses Rischin (Cambridge, MA, 1967), pp. 192–3.

39 M. Olgin, 'Di yidishe sprakh in undzer privat-lebn', in *Never Say Die!: A Thousand Years of Yiddish in Jewish Life and Letters*, ed. Joshua A. Fishman (The Hague, Paris, and New York, 1981), pp. 551–64.

40 William Z. Foster and Earl Browder, 'He Wrote His Name in the Hearts of the Masses', in *M. J. Olgin: Leader and Teacher* (New York, 1939), p. 5; biographical details from 'M. J. Olgin: 1878–1939', in *M. J. Olgin: Leader and Teacher*, pp. 3–4.

41 *Der Hamer* (May 1926), pp. 50–1.

42 M. J. Olgin, 'The Real World of Tomorrow', in *M. J. Olgin: Leader and Teacher*, p. 9.

43 Olgin, 'The Soviet Union and National Liberation', in *M. J. Olgin: Leader and Teacher*, pp. 26–31.

44 Olgin, 'First All-Union Congress of Soviet Writers', in *American Writers' Congress*, ed. Henry Hart (New York, 1935), p. 49.

45 Olgin, 'Jewish Reconstruction on the Order of the Day', in *M. J. Olgin: Leader and Teacher*, pp. 11–16.

46 Olgin, 'Jewish Youth Speaks', in *M. J. Olgin: Leader and Teacher*, p. 22.

47 Moses Rischin, *The Promised City: New York's Jews, 1870–1914* (Cambridge, MA, and London, 1977), p. 153.

48 Janet Flint, *The Prints of Louis Lozowick: A Catalogue Raisonné* (New York, 1982); John Bowlt, 'Introduction', in *Louis Lozowick: American Precisionist Retrospective, February 26–May 7, 1978* (catalogue) (Long Beach, 1978); Wendy Kaplan, ed., *Designing Modernity: The Arts of Reform and Persuasion 1885–1945* (New York, 1995).

49 Jacob Riis, *How the Other Half Lives: Studies Among the Tenements of New York* [1901] (New York, 1971), p. 49.

50 W.J.T. Mitchell's analysis of William Blake, in Mitchell, *Picture Theory: Essays on Verbal and Visual Representation* (Chicago, 1984), pp. 120–1.

51 Tamar Manor-Friedman, ed., *Workers and Revolutionaries: The Jewish Labor Movement* (Tel Aviv, 1994), p. 125; Frances K. Pohl, *In the Eye of the Storm. An Art of Conscience 1930–1970: Selections from the Collection of Philip J. & Suzanne Schiller* (San Francisco, 1995).

52 Isaac A. Hourwich, *Immigration and Labor: The Economic Aspects of European Immigration to the United States* (New York and London, 1912).

53 Albert J. Reiss, 'Introduction', to Louis Wirth, *On Cities and Social Life: Selected Papers* (Chicago, 1964), p. xxvii.

54 Isaac Hourwich, *Oysgevehlte shrifin* (New York, 1917), pp. 53–71.

55 *Ibid.*, p. 75.

56 Melech Epstein, *Profiles of Eleven*, pp. 131–2.

57 *Ibid.*, p. 165.

58 *Ibid.*, p. 258.

59 Hourwich, *Immigration and Labor*, pp. 353–61.

60 *Ibid.*, pp. 161–5.

61 Compare Melech Epstein, *Profiles of Eleven*, pp. 267–8.

62 *Ibid.*, p. 261.

63 *Ibid.*

64 A. G. Hays, *City Lawyers: The Autobiography of a Law Practice* (New York, 1942).

65 Hourwich, in *Oysgevehlte shrifin*, p. 137.

66 *Ibid.*, pp. 140ff.

67 Melech Epstein, *Profiles of Eleven*, p. 255.

68 *Ibid.*, p. 114.

69 'Barondess, Joseph', *Encyclopedia Judaica*, p. 255.

70 Melech Epstein, *Profiles of Eleven*, p. 134.

71 *Ibid.*, pp. 117–19.

72 *Ibid.*, p. 115.

73 *Ibid.*, p. 197.

74 Melech Epstein, *Pages from a Colorful Life*, pp. 56–7.

75 Jacob Magidow, 'Recollections of an Old Associate', in *Gewerkschaften: Jubilee Book*, ed. Lang and Feinstone, p. 31.

76 Howe, *World of Our Fathers*, p. 314.

77 N. Goldberg, *Geshikhte fun der yidisher arbeter-bavegung in de fareynikte shtatn*, II, ed. E. Tscherikower, pp. 313ff.

78 Rischin, *The Promised City*, p. 154.

79 Howe, *World of Our Fathers*, p. 315.

80 Melech Epstein, *Profiles of Eleven*, pp. 164–5.

81 Michael Berkowitz, *Zionist Culture and West European Jewry Before the First World War* (Cambridge, 1993), pp. 8–39.

82 Melech Epstein, *Profiles of Eleven*, p. 164.

83 Harry Rogoff, *An East Side Epic: The Life and Work of Meyer London* (New York, 1930), pp. 172–3.

84 Howe, *World of Our Fathers*, p. 295.

85 *Ibid.*, p. 297.

86 Part of the reason may be that few of the leading labour historians work in Yiddish-language sources. See Gwendolyn Mink, *Old Labor and New Immigrants in American Political Development: Union, Party, and State, 1875–1920* (Ithaca, 1986); compare Julie Greene, *Pure and Simple: The American Federation of Labor and Political Activism, 1881–1917* (Cambridge, 1998).

87 Howe, *World of Our Fathers*, p. 315.

88 Marx Lewis, *Meyer London* (New York, 1975), p. 16.

89 Melech Epstein, *Profiles of Eleven*, pp. 170–1.

90 Marx Lewis, *Meyer London*, p. 17.

91 'In Memoriam', in *Gewerkschaften: Jubilee Book*, ed. Lang and Feinstone, p. 62.

92 Illus. 98, from Baruch Charney Vladeck, *B. Vladeck in lebn un shafen*, ed. Yefim Yeshurin (New York, 1936).

93 *Leksikon fun der noyer yidisher literatur* (New York, 1960), pp. 469–75.

94 'Der yonger Lasalle in New York', *Forverts*, 3 December 1908, facsimile in Vladeck, *Vladeck in lebn un shafen*, p. 46.

95 'In Memoriam', p. 62.

96 *Vladeck Houses* (New York, 1940).

97 Dr Ernest Oliveri provided this insight.

98 Leon Shapiro, *The History of ORT: A Jewish Movement for Social Change* (New York, 1980).

99 'In Memoriam', p. 62.

100 Melech Epstein, *Profiles of Eleven*, p. 326.

101 'Moshe Rabeinu', in Vladeck, *Vladeck in lebn un shafen*, pp. 183–216.

102 Melech Epstein, *Profiles of Eleven*, p. 326.

103 *Ibid.*, pp. 343–5.

104 *Ibid.*, p. 346.

105 'Cahan, Abraham (1860–1951)', *Encyclopaedia Judaica*, p. 14.

106 Rischin, *The Promised City*, p. 124.

107 'Cahan', *Encyclopaedia Judaica*, p. 15.

108 Melech Epstein, *Profiles of Eleven*, pp. 78–9.

109 Maximillian Hurwitz, *The Workmen's Circle: Its History, Ideals, Organization and Institutions* (New York, 1936), pp. 105–7.

110 Melech Epstein, *Pages from a Colorful Life*, p. 50; see Frankel, *Prophecy and Politics*, pp. 506–7, for an amusing critical view.

111 Hillel [Harry] Rogoff, *Der gayst fun Forverts* [The Spirit of the *Forward*] (New York, 1954).

112 B. Charney Vladeck, 'The Gewerkschaften Celebrates a Half-Century', in *Gewerkschaften: Jubilee Book*, ed. Lang and Feinstone, p. 63.

113 Morris C. Feinstone, 'A Brief History of the United Hebrew Trades', in *Gewerkschaften: Jubilee Book*, ed. Lang and Feinstone, p. 19.

114 *Ibid.*, pp. 13–14.

115 Introduction to *Gewerkschaften: Jubilee Book*, ed. Lang and Feinstone, pp. 4–5.

116 Feinstone, 'Brief History', pp. 26–7.

117 See Aaron R. Rollin, 'Bletlekh tsu der geshikhte fun der yidisher arbeter-baveg-ung in England', and Jacob Hodess, 'Tsu der geshikhte fun der english-yiddish presse', both in *Yidn in England: studies un materialn 1880–1940* (New York, 1940), pp. 273–82, 40–71; Fishman, *East End Jewish Radicals*.

118 Kershen, *Uniting the Tailors*, p. xviii.

119 Manny Shinwell, *Lead with the Left: My First Ninety-Six Years* (London, 1981), pp. 169–71; Peter Slowe, *Manny Shinwell: An Authorised Biography* (London and Boulder, 1993), pp. 182–3.

120 Elise Janner, *Barnett Janner: A Personal Portrait*, ed. Gershom Levi (London, 1984), p. 34.

121 *Ibid.*, p. 48.

122 Reg Kray and Ron Kray with Fred Dinenage, *Our Story* (London, 1989), p. 12.

123 James Morton, *Gangland: London's Underworld* (London, 1998), p. 38.

124 John Harding with Jack Kid Berg, *Jack Kid Berg: The Whitechapel Windmill* (London, 1987), p. 78.

125 See Philip Roth, *American Pastoral* (London, 1998), p. 20.

Epilogue

1 Moses Rischin, *The Promised City: New York's Jews, 1870–1914* (Cambridge, MA, and London, 1977), p. 155.

2 'Briscoe, Robert' in *Dictionary of Jewish Biography*, ed. Geoffrey Wigoder (New York, 1991), p. 84.

Select Bibliography

Archives and libraries

American Jewish Archives, Cincinnati, OH
American Jewish Historical Society, Waltham, MA
Bodleian Library, University of Oxford
British Library, London
Central Zionist Archives, Jerusalem
Hadassah Archives, New York
Jewish Museum, Finchley, London
Jewish National Library, Jerusalem
Klau Library, Hebrew Union College – Jewish Institute of Religion, Cincinnati, OH
Leo Baeck Institute, New York
London School of Economics and Political Science (LSE) Library
New York Public Library
Ohio State University Libraries, Columbus, OH
Regenstein Library, University of Chicago
Rosenberger Collection, University of Chicago
School of Oriental and African Studies (SOAS) Library, London
Senate House Library, University of London
Tel Aviv University Library
University College London Library
University of Amsterdam Library
Wiener Library, Tel Aviv
YIVO (Yiddish Scientific Research Institute), New York

Primary sources

PERIODICALS

American Hebrew
American Jewish Historical Quarterly
Arbeter Fraynd
Aufbau: jüdische illustrierte Zeitung
Avukah Annual
Avukah Bulletin
Blau-Weiss Blätter
Blau-Weiss Brille
Boston Hebrew
Forward
Frayhayt
Freiheit
Hadassah Bulletin
Hadassah News Letter
Der Hamer
Jerubbaal
Jewish Academy
Jewish Chronicle
Jewish Criterion
Jewish Tribune
Der Jude
Der jüdische Pfadfinder
Jüdische Rundschau
Der jüdische Student

Jüdische Turnzeitung
Der Jüdische Wille
Jüdischer Nationalkalendar
Karnanu
Kinder tshurnal
Korrespondenzblatt des Verbandes
	Jüdischer Frauen für Palästina Arbeit
Maccabaean
Magazine of the Inter-University Jewish
	Federation of Great Britain and
	Ireland
Manchester Guardian
Menorah
Monthly Pioneer
Morgen frayhayt
Neue jüdische Monatshefte
Der neue Weg
New Judaea
New Maccabbaean
New Palestine
New York Times
La Nouvelle Aurore

Ost und West
Our Fund
Palästina Aufbau
Palästina-Bilder-Korrespondenz
Palästina Fragen
Palestine Pictorial Service
Palestine Progress
Palestine Weekly
Pioneer
Pioneers and Helpers
Pioniere und Helfer
Social Research
Der Tag
Die Tat
Tsukunft
Volk und Land
Die Welt
Yedioth Hadassah
Young Judaean
Young Zionist
Zionist Free Press

BOOKS, PAMPHLETS, ARTICLES

Adler, Eleanor H. 'Child Flower-Makers in New York Tenements'. *Child Labor Bulletin*, III/4 (February 1915), pp. 17–18

Arbeiterinnen Erzählen: Kampf und Leben in Eretz Israel. Berlin, 1935

Arlosoroff-Goldberg, Gerda. *Palästina Fragen.* Zurich, 1929

Auerbach, Elias. *Palästina als Judenland.* Berlin and Leipzig, 1912

Der Aufbau des jüdischen Palästina. Berlin, 1922

Der Aufbau Palästinas und das deutsche Judentum: Reden–Aufsätze–Dokumente. Berlin, 1922

Benjamin, Walter. *Charles Baudelaire: A Lyric Poet in the Age of High Capitalism.* Trans. Harry Zohn and Quentin Hoare. London, 1973

——. 'Theses on the Philosophy of History'. In *Illuminations*, ed. Hannah Arendt, trans. Harry Zohn, pp. 253–64. New York, 1968

——. 'The Work of Art in the Age of Mechanical Reproduction'. In *Illuminations*, ed. Hannah Arendt, trans. Harry Zohn, pp. 217–51. New York, 1968

——, and Gershom Scholem. *The Correspondence of Walter Benjamin and Gershom Scholem, 1932–1938.* Trans. Gary Smith and Andre Lefevere, intro. Anson Rabinbach. New York, 1989

Benor-Kalter, Yaakov. *Photographs of the New Working Palestine.* Haifa, 1935

Bergmann, Hugo. *Jawne und Jerusalem.* Berlin, 1919

Berkman, Alexander. *Gefengnis-erinerungen fun an anarkhist* [Prison Memoirs of an Anarchist]. Trans. M. Katts and A. Frumkin. New York, 1920–21

Bernstein, Herman, ed. *Celebrities of Our Time.* London, 1924

Birnbaum, Nathan. *Im Dienste der Verheissung.* Frankfurt a.M., 1927

Blau-Weiss Führer: Leitfaden für die Arbeit im Jud. Wanderbund 'Blau-Weiss'. Berlin, 5677/1917

Blau-Weiss Liederbuch. Berlin, 1914

Boehm, Adolf. *The Jewish National Fund.* The Hague, n.d.

——. *Der Palästina-Aufbaufonds (Keren Hajessod)*. London, 1925

——. *Die zionistische Bewegung*. Tel Aviv, 1935–7

——. *Die zionistische Bewegung bis zum Ende des Weltkrieges I*, 2nd edn. Berlin, 1915

Brandeis, Louis D. *Half Brother, Half Son: The Letters of Louis D. Brandeis to Felix Frankfurter*. Ed. Melvin Urofsky and David Levy. Norman, OK, 1991

——. *Jewish Rights and the Congress: Address Delivered at Carnegie Hall, New York City, January 24, 1916*. New York, 1916

——. *Letters of Louis D. Brandeis*, vols 1–5. Ed. Melvin Urofsky and David Levy. Albany, 1971–8

——. *Zionism and Patriotism*. New York, 1915

Britton, Wiley. *The White Slavery: A Study of the Present Trade Union System*. Akron, OH, 1909

Buber, Martin. *A Land of Two Peoples: Martin Buber on Jews and Arabs*. Ed. Paul Mendes-Flohr. New York, 1983

Cahan, Abraham. *The Education of Abraham Cahan*. Trans. Leon Stein, Abraham P. Conan and Lynn Davison. Philadelphia, 1969

——. *Grandma Never Lived in America: The New Journalism of Abraham Cahan*. Ed. Moses Rischin. Bloomington, 1985

——. *The Rise of David Levinsky: A Novel*. New York and London, 1917

——. *Yekl, A Tale of the New York Ghetto*. New York, 1899

Cohen, Israel, ed. *Speeches on Zionism by Balfour*. London, 1928

——, ed. *Zionist Work in Palestine by Various Authorities*. Westport, CT, 1976

Donath, Adolph. *Hermann Struck*. Berlin, 1920

Dugdale, Blanche. *Arthur James Balfour*. New York, 1937

Dyche, John A. *Bolshevism in American Labor Unions: A Plea for Constructive Unionism*. New York, 1926

Einstein, Albert. *About Zionism*. Ed. and trans. Leon Simon. London, 1930

Eisenstadt, Benzion. *Hakhme Yisrael ba-Amerika* [Wise Men of Israel in America]. New York, 1903

Epstein, Elias M. *The Case for the Jewish National Fund: A Challenge to Zionists*. Jerusalem, 1928

Epstein, Melech. *Pages from a Colorful Life: An Autobiographical Sketch*. Miami Beach, 1971

Fischman, Ada. *Die Arbeitende Frau in Erez Israel: Geschichte der Arbeiterinnen-bewegung in Palästina 1904–1930*. Tel Aviv, 1930

Fortlage, Arnold and Karl Schwarz, *Das graphische Werk von Hermann Struck*. Berlin, 1911

Gassman-Sherr, Rosalie. *The Story of the Federation of Women Zionists of Great Britain and Ireland, 1918–1968*. London, 1968

Goldman, Emma. *Anarchism and Other Essays* [1917]. New York, 1969

Goldmann, Nahum. *The Autobiography of Nahum Goldman: Sixty Years of Jewish Life*. Trans. Helen Serba. New York, 1969

Gordon, A. *Briefe aus Palästina*. Berlin, 1919

The Greatest Romance in History. New York, 1922

Grove-Pollak, Fay, ed. *The Saga of a Movement: WIZO 1920–1970*. N.p., n.d.

De Haas, Jacob. *Theodor Herzl: A Biographical Study*, 2 vols. Chicago and New York, 1927

Handbook of Trade Union Methods with Special Reference to the Garment Trades. New York, 1937

Hapgood, Hutchins. *The Spirit of the Ghetto* [1902]. Ed. Moses Rischin. Cambridge, MA, 1967

Harding, John, with Jack 'Kid' Berg. *Jack Kid Berg: The Whitechapel Windmill*.

London, 1987

Harry, Myriam. *A Springtide in Palestine*. London, 1924

Hart, Henry, ed. *American Writers' Congress*. New York, 1935

Hays, A. G. *City Lawyers: The Autobiography of a Law Practice*. New York, 1942

Heller, Max. *My Month in Palestine: Impressions of Travel*. New York, 1929

Hertz, Y. S. *Fuftzig yor arbeter-ring in yidishn lebn* [Fifty Years of the Workmen's Circle in Jewish Life]. New York, 1950

Herzl, Theodor. *Altneuland*. Leipzig, 1902

——. *The Complete Diaries of Theodor Herzl*, 5 vols. Ed. Raphael Patai, trans. Harry Zohn. New York, 1960

——. *Der Judenstaat: Versuch einer modernen Loesung der Judenfrage*. Leipzig and Vienna, 1896

——. *Theodor Herzls zionistische Schriften*. Berlin, 1908

——. *Zionist Writings*. 2 vols. Trans. Harry Zohn. New York, 1973–5

Hillquit, Morris. *From Marx to Lenin*. New York, 1921

——. *History of Socialism in the United States*, 5th edn. New York, 1971

——. *Loose Leaves from a Busy Life*. New York, 1934

——. *Present-Day Socialism*. New York, [c. 1920]

——. *Recent Progress of the Socialist and Labor Movements in the United States*. Chicago, 1907

——. *Socialism in Theory and Practice*. New York, 1909

——. *Socialism on Trial*. New York, 1920

——. *Socialism Summed Up*. New York, 1913

——, Samuel Gompers, and Max S. Hayes. *The Double Edge of Labor's Sword: Discussion and Testimony on Socialism and Trade-Unionism Before the Commission on Industrial Relations*. Chicago, 1914

——, and John A. Ryan. *Socialism: Promise or Menace?* New York, 1914

Hine, Lewis. *Lewis Hine. Passionate Journey: Photographs 1905–1937*. Ed. Karl Steinorth. Rochester, NY, 1996

Hirschberg, Heinrich. *Der Humor bei Struck*. Berlin, 1919

Hourwich, Isaac. *The Case of Russia*. New York, 1905

——. *The Economic Aspects of Immigration*. Washington, DC, 1912

——. *The Economics of the Russian Village* [1892]. New York, 1972

——. *Immigration and Labor: The Economic Aspects of European Immigration to the United States*. New York and London, 1912

——. *Oysgevehlte shriftn* [Selected Writings]. New York, 1917

——, Albert Sidney Bolles, Frederick Albert Cleveland, Charles A. Conant, F. R. Fairchild, Edward Sherwood Meade, Charles S. Potts and Frank Maloy Anderson (corporate author: American Academy of Political and Social Science). *Problems in Banking and Finance*. Philadelphia, 1902

Howe, Irving. *A Margin of Hope: An Intellectual Autobiography*. New York, 1982

Hurwitz, Maximillian. *The Workmen's Circle: Its History, Ideals, Organization and Institutions*. New York, 1936

Jabotinsky, Vladimir. *Die jüdischer Legion im Weltkrieg*. Berlin, 1930

——. *Turkey and the War*. London, 1917

Janner, Elise. *Barnett Janner: A Personal Portrait*. Ed. Gershom Levi. London, 1984

Janovsky, Saul Joseph. *Ershte yorn fun yidishn fayhaytlekhn sotsializm, oytobiografishe zikhroynes fun a pioner un boyer fun der yidisher anarkhistisher bavegung in England un Amerke* [First Years of Jewish Libertine Socialism, Autobiographical Reminiscences of a Pioneer and Builder of the Yiddish Anarchist Movement in England and America]. New York, 1948

——. *Sh. Yanovski: zayn lebn, kemfn un shafn, 1864–1939* [Life, Struggles, and

Work]. Ed. Abba Gordin. Los Angeles, 1957

Jeshurin, Ephim H., ed. *B. C. Vladeck: Fifty Years of Life and Labor*. New York, 1936

Jewish Progress in Palestine: Four Years' Work of Keren Hayesod. London, 1925

Jüdischer Almanach 11. Ed. Berthold Fiewel. Berlin, 1904

Jüdischer Almanach 5670: Bar-Kochba in Wien. Cologne, 1910

Jüdischer Nationalkalender 5676. Berlin, 1915–16

Jüdisches Archiv. Vienna, 1915

Kadimah. New York, 1918

Kallen, Horrace. 'Julian Mack 1866–1943'. *American Jewish Year Book* 46 (1944), pp. 35–46

Katznelson-Shazar, Rachel, ed. *The Plough Woman: Records of the Pioneer Women of Palestine*. Trans. Maurice Samuel. New York, 1932

Der Keren Hajessod: Verfassung und Programm. London, 1922

Keren Hayesod (Palestine Foundation Fund): What It Has Done, What It Has to Do, and What You Should Do. Keren Hayesod Committee of the English Zionist Federation, *c*. 1922

King, Edward. *Joseph Zalmonah*. Boston, 1893

Kohut, Rebekah. *My Portion (An Autobiography)*. New York, 1925

Kray, Reg and Ron Kray, with Fred Dinenage. *Our Story*. London, 1989

Kurtz, Aaron. *Moshe Olgin*. Cleveland, 1940

Landauer, Gustav. *Oifruf tsum sotsializm* [Call to Socialism]. Trans. H. Frank and B. Rosenthal. Berlin, 1920

Lang, Harry and Morris Feinstone, eds. *Gewerkschaften*. New York, 1928

——. *Gewerkschaften: Jubilee Book*. New York, 1938

Leksikon fun der noyer yidisher literatur. New York, 1960

Levinger, Elma. *Fighting Angel*. New York, 1946

Liessin, Abraham. *Lider und poemen*. New York, 1938

——. *Zikhroynes un bilder* [Memoirs and Pictures]. New York, 1954

Lilien, E. M. [illustrator]. *Die Bibel: in Auswahl fürs Haus mit Zeichnungen von E. M. Lilien, Martin Luther Translation*. Ed. E. Lehmann and [n.i.] Petersen. Braunschweig and Berlin, n.d.

——. *The Holy Land*. Berlin and Vienna, 1922

Lindheim, Irma. *The Immortal Adventure*. New York, 1928

——. *Parallel Quest: A Search of a Person and a People*. New York, 1962

Lipsky, Louis. *Memoirs in Profile*. Philadelphia, 1975

M. J. Olgin: Leader and Teacher. New York, 1939

M. Olgin Albom. New York, 1941

Magidoff, Jacob. *Des shpigel fun der ist sayd* [The Mirror of the East Side]. New York, 1923

Magnes, Judah L. *Dissenter in Zion*. Ed. Arthur A. Goren. Cambridge, MA, and London, 1988

Most, Johann [John]. *The Deistic Pestilence and the Religious Plague of Man*. N.p., 1880

——. *Die Freie Gesellschaft. Eine Abhandlung über Principien und Taktik der kommunistischen Anarchisten: nebst einem polemischen Anhang*. New York, 1884

——. *Der komunistisher anarkhizm*. Trans. Rudolf Rocker. London, 1906

Das neue Palästina. Berlin, 1921

Niger, S. *Dertseylers un romanistn* [Short-Story Writers and Novelists]. New York, 1946

Nordau, Anna and Max Nordau. *Max Nordau: A Biography*. New York, 1943

Nordau, Max. *Max Nordaus zionistische Schriften*. Cologne and Leipzig, 1909

Palästina Aufbau. Jerusalem, 1928

Palästina Aufbau und Frauenarbeit. London, n.d.

Palästina und der Neubeginn jüdischen Lebens. Berlin, n.d.

Palestine During the War: Being a Record of the Preservation of the Jewish Settlement in Palestine. London, 1921

Patterson, J. H. *With the Judaeans in the Palestine Campaign.* London, 1922

——. *With the Zionists in Gallipoli.* New York, 1916

Peretz, Isaac Lieb. *Di verk fun Yitsak Yabush Perez.* Ed. David Pinski. New York, 1920

Pinski, David. *Naye ertsehlungen* [New Stories]. Berlin, 1923

Program for American Jews. New York, 1938

Raisin, Max. *A History of the Jews in Modern Times,* 5th edn. New York, 1937

Report of the Emergency Fund for Palestine September 1, 1929–December 31, 1934. Jerusalem, 1936

Report of the Reorganization Commission of the Executive of the Zionist Organization on the Work of the Zionist Organization in Palestine. New York, 1921

Riis, Jacob A. *How the Other Half Lives: Studies Among the Tenements of New York* [1901]. New York, 1971

Rocker, Rudolf. *Hinter shtekhige droht un grates: erinerungen fun der krigs-gefangenshaft in england* [Behind Barbed-Wire: Memories of a Wartime Prisoner in England]. Trans. A. Frumkin. New York, 1927

——. *The London Years.* Trans. Joseph Leftwich. London, 1956

Rogoff, Harry [Hillel]. *An East Side Epic: The Life and Work of Meyer London.* New York, 1930

——. *Der gayst fun Forverts* [The Spirit of the *Forward*]. New York, 1954

Rosenberger, Erwin. *Herzl as I Remember Him.* Trans. Louis Jay Hermann. New York, 1959

Ross, Barney and Martin Abramson, *No Man Stands Alone.* London, 1959

Ruppin, Arthur. *Der Aufbau des Landes Israel.* Berlin, 1919

——. *The Jews in the Modern World.* London, 1934

Sampter, Jessie. *A Course in Zionism.* New York, 1915

Sankowsky, Shoshana Harris. *Short History of Zionism.* No. 3 Avukah Program. 1936

Schneiderman, Rose with Lucy Goldthwaite. *All for One.* New York, 1967

Scholem, Gershom. *From Berlin to Jerusalem: Memories of My Youth.* Trans. Harry Zohn. New York, 1980

——. 'Jüdische Jugendbewegung'. *Der Jude* (March 1917), pp. 822–4

Shinwell, Manny. *Lead with the Left: My First Ninety-Six Years.* London, 1981

Should Socialism Prevail? A Debate Held October 21, 1915, Brooklyn, New York Under the Auspices of the Brooklyn Institute of Arts and Sciences. Subject: Resolved. That Socialism Ought to Prevail in the United States. Affirmative: Professor Scott Nearing, Mr. Morris Hillquit; Negative: Rev. Dr. John L. Belford, Professor Frederick M. Davenport; J. Herbert Lowe, Chairman. New York, 1916

Sieff, Israel. *Memoirs.* London, 1970

Simon, Julius. *Certain Days.* Ed. Evyatar Friesel. Jerusalem, 1971

Soule, George. *Sidney Hillman: Labor Statesman.* New York, 1939

Stein, Nadia. *Women in Eretz Israel.* Trans. D. C. Adler Hobman. London, 1927

Stenographisches Protokoll der Verhandlungen des VIII. Zionisten-Kongress in Haag vom 14. bis inklusive 21. August 1907. Cologne, 1907

Straus, Rahel. 'The Importance of Our Work for the Promotion of Health in Palestine', in *Report of the Jewish Women's League for Cultural Work in Palestine for 1913.* N.p., n.d.

——. *Wir lebten in Deutschland: Erinnerungen einer deutschen Jüdin, 1880–1933.* Stuttgart, 1962

Struck, Hermann. *Palästina: Reisebilder.* Berlin, 1904

Szold, Henrietta. *Henrietta Szold: Life and Letters.* Ed. Marvin Lowenthal. New

York, 1942

Die Tätigkeit des Wiener Palästina-Amtes. N.p., 1922

Tätigkeitsbericht 1929–31 an die VI. Konferenz in Basel. 22–28 Juni 1931. Women's
International Zionist Organization.

Thieberger, Friedrich and Felix Weltsch, eds. *Jüdischer Almanach auf das Jahr 5691.*
Prague, 1930

Thomashevsky, Bessie. *Mayn lebns-geshikhte* [My Life Story]. New York, 1916

Ulitzur, A. *Two Decades of Keren Hayesod: A Survey in Facts and Figures 1921–1940.*
Jerusalem, 1940

Vladeck, Baruch Charney. *B. Vladeck in lebn un shafen* [Life and Work]. Ed. Yefim
Yeshurin. New York, 1936

——, ed. *Fun der tiefenish fun harz* [From the Depths of the Heart]. New York, 1917

Vladeck Houses. New York, 1940

Wald, Lillian D. *The House on Henry Street.* New York, 1915

——. *Windows in Henry Street.* Boston, 1934

Warburg, Aby. *Images from the Region of the Pueblo Indians of North America.* Trans.
and ed. Michael P. Steinberg. Ithaca and London, 1995

Weizmann, Chaim. *The Letters and Papers of Chaim Weizmann II.* Gen. ed., Meyer
Weisgal. London, 1971

——. *Trial and Error: The Autobiography of Chaim Weizmann.* New York, 1966

Weizmann der Führer: Anlässlich seines Besuches in Brünn im Januar 1925. Prague [?],
1925

Who's Who in WIZO 1966–1970. Tel Aviv, 1970

Winchevsky, Morris. *Gezamlte Verk.* Ed. Kalman Marmor. New York, 1927–8

——. *Der meshugener filozof in england: tsushlogene gedanken, bilder, verter un hakires,
dem filozofs lebens-geshikhte* [The Meshugener Philosopher in England: Tacked-on
Thought, Pictures, Verses and Speculations of the Philosopher's Life Story]. New
York, 1920

Wise, Stephen. *Challenging Years: The Autobiography of Stephen Wise.* New York, 1949

[*Stephen S.*] *Wise. Servant of the People: Selected Letters.* Ed. Carl Voss. Philadelphia,
1969

*Women's International Zionist Organization: Report for the Period 1923–1925 for the
Women's International Zionist Conference.* N.p., n.d.

Workmen's Circle, Ephim H. Jeshurin, and Jacob Sholem Hertz. *Arbeter Ring: boyer
un tuer* [Workmen's Circle: Pioneers and Builders]. New York, 1962

Zangwill, Israel. *Speeches, Articles, and Letters of Israel Zangwill.* Ed. Maurice Simon.
London, 1937

Zhitlowsky, Chaim. *Gezamlte shriftn.* Warsaw, c. 1931–5

——. *Yidn un yidishkayt.* New York, 1939

Zweig, Arnold. *De Vriendt Goes Home.* Trans. Eric Sutton. New York, 1933

——, and Hermann Struck. *Das ostjüdische Antlitz* [1920]. Wiesbaden, 1988

Secondary sources

PERIODICALS AND
COLLECTED WORKS

AJS Review
American Historical Review
American Jewish Historical Quarterly
American Jewish Year Book

American Sociological Review
Bol'shaia sovetskaia entsiklopediia
Bulletin des Leo Baeck Instituts
Encyclopaedia Judaica

English Historical Review
German Quarterly
German Studies Review
Historische Zeitschrift
Jerusalem Cathedre
Jerusalem Quarterly
Jewish Social Studies
Journal of Contemporary History
Journal of Israel History
Journal of Jewish Sociology
Journal of Modern History
Journal of the American Academy of
    Religion
Journal of Women's History
Judaism

LBI News
Modern Judaism
New German Critique
Representations
Shofar
Signs
Studies in Contemporary Jewry
Studies in Zionism
Wiener Library Bulletin
Year Book of the Leo Baeck Institute
Zion
HaZionut
Z'manim

BOOKS, CHAPTERS, ARTICLES

Adam, Peter. *Art as Politics in the Third Reich*. New York, 1992

Alderman, Geoffrey. *The Jewish Community in British Politics*. Oxford, 1983

——. *Modern British Jewry*. Oxford, 1992

Almog, Schmuel. *Zionism and History: The Rise of a New Jewish Consciousness*. New York, 1987

Altschuler, M. 'Russia and Her Jews – The Impact of the 1914 War'. *Wiener Library Bulletin*, 27 (1973/4), pp. 12–16

Amit, M. *ha-Meri: perakim mi-ma'avak ha-kiyum shel ha-Yahadut ha-haredit be-erets-Yisrael* [The Uprising: Chapters from the Struggle of the Existence of Hardi Jewry in the Land of Israel]. Bene Beraq, c. 1982

Anderson, Benedict. *Imagined Communities: Reflections on the Origin and Spread of Nationalism*. London, 1983

Appleby, R. Scott, ed. *Spokesmen for the Despised: Fundamentalist Leaders of the Middle East*. London and Chicago, 1997

Archdeacon, Thomas J. *Becoming American: An Ethnic History*. New York and London, 1983

Aschheim, Steven E. *Brothers and Strangers: East European Jews in German and German–Jewish Consciousness, 1800–1923*. Madison, WI, 1982

Avineri, Shlomo. *The Making of Modern Zionism: The Intellectual Origins of the Jewish State*. New York, 1981

Avrich, Paul. *Anarchist Portraits*. Princeton, 1990

——. *Anarchist Voices: An Oral History of Anarchists in America*. Princeton, 1988

Barnard, Harry. *The Forging of an American Jew: The Life and Times of Judge Julian W. Mack*. New York, 1974

Baron, Lawrence. 'Erich Muehsam's Jewish Identity'. *Year Book of the Leo Baeck Institute*, XXV (1980), pp. 269–84

Barthes, Roland. *Image–Music–Text*. Trans. Stephen Heath. New York, 1977

Baskin, Judith R., ed. *Jewish Women in Historical Perspective*. Detroit, 1991

Beloff, Halla. *Camera Culture*. New York, 1985

Ben-Asher, Naomi. *Great Jewish Women Throughout History: A Course of Study in Seven Outlines*. New York, 1954

Ben-Horin, Meir. *Max Nordau: Philosopher of Human Solidarity*. London, 1956

Ben-Yehudah, Nachman. *Political Assassinations by Jews: A Rhetorical Device for*

Justice. Albany, 1993

Berger, John. *Ways of Seeing*. London, 1987

van den Bergh, Govaert C.J.J. *De taal zegt meer dan zij verantwoorden kan* [Language Contains More than Can Be Accounted for]. Nijmegen, 1994

Berkowitz, Joel. 'Shakespeare on the American Yiddish Stage'. PhD dissertation, City University of New York, 1995

Berkowitz, Michael. *Western Jewry and the Zionist Project, 1914–1933*. Cambridge, 1997

———. *Zionist Culture and West European Jewry Before the First World War*. Cambridge, 1993

Berman, Aaron. *Nazism, the Jews and American Zionism, 1933–1948*. Detroit, 1990

Berman, Russell. *Cultural Studies of Modern Germany: History, Representation, and Nationhood*. Madison, WI, 1993

———. *Modern Culture and Critical Theory: Art, Politics, and the Legacy of the Frankfurt School*. Madison, WI, 1988

Bernstein, Deborah, ed. *Pioneers and Homemakers: Jewish Women in Pre-State Israel*. Albany, 1992

———. *The Struggle for Equality: Urban Women Workers in Prestate Israeli Society*. New York, 1987

Betz, Albrecht. 'Commodity and Modernity in Heine and Benjamin'. *New German Critique*, 33 (Fall 1984), pp. 179–88

Biale, David. *Eros and the Jews: From Biblical Israel to Contemporary America*. New York, 1992

———. *Gershom Scholem: Kabbalah and Counter-History*. Cambridge, MA, 1979

———. *Power and Powerlessness in Jewish History*. New York, 1987

Black, Eugene C. *The Social Politics of Anglo–Jewry 1880–1920*. Oxford, 1988

Blau, Joseph *et al.*, eds. *Essays on Jewish Life and Thought: Presented in Honor of Salo Wittmayer Baron*. New York, 1959

Bloch, Marc. *The Historian's Craft*. Trans. Peter Putnam. New York, 1953

Boyarin, Jonathan, and Daniel Boyarin, eds. *Jews and Other Differences: The New Jewish Cultural Studies*. Minneapolis and London, 1997

Breines, Paul. *Tough Jews: Political Fantasies and the Moral Dilemma of American Jewry*. New York, 1990

Bremner, Robert H. *American Philanthropy*, 2nd edn. Chicago, 1988

Brennan, Teresa and Martin Jay, eds. *Vision in Context: Historical and Contemporary Perspectives on Sight*. New York and London, 1996

Brenner, David. 'Marketing Identities: The Invention of Jewish Ethnicity'. In *Ost und West*. Detroit, 1998

Brenner, Michael. *The Renaissance of Jewish Culture in Weimar Germany*. New Haven, 1995

Breuer, Mordechai. *Modernity Within Tradition: The Social History of Orthodox Jewry in Imperial Germany*. Trans. Elizabeth Petuchowski. New York, 1992

Bristow, Edward J. *Prostitution and Prejudice: The Jewish Fight Against White Slavery, 1870–1933*. New York, 1983

Brown, Michael. *The Israeli–American Connection: Its Roots in the Yishuv, 1914–1945*. Detroit, 1997

Buck-Morss, Susan. *The Dialectics of Seeing: Walter Benjamin and the Arcades Project*. Cambridge, MA, and London, 1989

Buhle, Paul, ed. *History and the New Left: Madison, Wisconsin, 1950–1970*. Philadelphia, 1990

Burt, Robert A. *Two Jewish Justices: Outcasts in the Promised Land*. Berkeley, 1988

Caplan, Neil. 'Zionist Visions in the Early 1930s'. *Studies in Contemporary Jewry*, IV

(1988), pp. 232–49

Cassedy, Steven. *To the Other Shore: The Russian Jewish Intellectuals Who Came to America*. Princeton, 1997

Cesarani, David. *The Jewish Chronicle and Anglo–Jewry, 1841–1991*. Cambridge, 1994

——, ed. *The Making of Modern Anglo–Jewry*. Oxford, 1990

——. 'Zionism in England, 1917–1939'. PhD dissertation, University of Oxford, 1986

Chartier, Roger. 'Texts, Printing, Readings'. In *The New Cultural History*, ed. Lynn Hunt, pp. 154–75. Berkeley, 1989

Cheyette, Bryan. *Constructions of 'The Jew' in English Literature and Society: Racial Representations 1875–1945*. Cambridge, 1993

Clifford, James. *The Predicament of Culture: Twentieth-Century Ethnography, Literature, and Art*. London and Cambridge, MA, 1988

Cohen, Mitchell. *Zion and State: Nation, Class, and the Shaping of Modern Israel*. Oxford, 1987

Cohen, Naomi W. *American Jews and the Zionist Idea*. New York, 1975

——. *The Year After the Riots: American Responses to the Palestine Crisis of 1929–30*. Detroit, 1988

Cohen, Richard I. *Jewish Icons: Art and Society in Modern Europe*. Berkeley, 1998

Cohen, Stuart A. *English Zionists and British Jews: The Communal Politics of Anglo–Jewry 1895–1920*. Princeton, 1982

Dash, Joan. *Summoned to Jerusalem: The Life of Henrietta Szold*. New York, 1979

Davidman, Lynn and Shelly Tennenbaum, eds. *Feminist Perspectives on Jewish Studies*. New Haven and London, 1994

Dawson, Nelson L., ed. *Brandeis and America*. Lexington, KY, 1989

Degler, Carl. *Out of Our Past: The Forces That Shaped Modern America*, rev. edn. New York, 1970

Ecksteins, Modris. *Rites of Spring: The Great War and the Birth of the Modern Age*. London, 1990

Edelheit, Abraham. *The Yishuv in the Shadow of the Holocaust*. Boulder, 1997

Efron, John. *Defenders of the Race: Jewish Doctors and Race Science in Fin-de-Siècle Europe*. New Haven, 1994

Elon, Amos. *Herzl*. New York, 1975

——. *The Israelis: Founders and Sons*. New York, 1981

Epstein, A. L. *Ethos and Identity*. London, 1978

Epstein, Melech. *Profiles of Eleven: Profiles of Eleven Men Who Guided The Destiny of an Immigrant Society and Stimulated Social Consciousness Among the American People*. Detroit, 1965

Feingold, Henry L. *The Jewish People in America, vol. V. A Time for Searching: Entering the Mainstream 1920–1945*. Baltimore and London, 1992

Feldman, David. *Englishmen and Jews: Social Relations and Political Culture, 1840–1914*. New Haven, 1994

Fineman, Irving. *Woman of Valor*. New York, 1961

Finkielkraut, Alain. *The Imaginary Jew*. Trans. Kevin O'Neil and David Suchoff. Lincoln, NE, 1994

Fischer, Michael M. J. 'Ethnicity and the Post-Modern Arts of Memory'. In *Writing Culture: The Poetics and Politics of Ethnography*, ed. James Clifford and George E. Marcus, pp. 194–233. Berkeley, 1986

Fischer, Roger. *Tippecanoe and Trinkets Too: The Material Culture of American Presidential Campaigns, 1828–1924*. Urbana and Chicago, 1988

Fishman, Joshua A. *Ideology, Society, and Language: The Odyssey of Nathan Birnbaum*. Ann Arbor, 1987

——, ed. *Never Say Die!: A Thousand Years of Yiddish in Jewish Life and Letters*. The Hague, Paris, and New York, 1981

Fishman, William J. *East End Jewish Radicals, 1875–1914*. London, 1975

——. 'Morris Winchevsky's London Yiddish Newspaper: One Hundred Years in Retrospect'. Second Annual Avrom-Nokhem Stencl Lecture in Modern Yiddish Literature, delivered 9 August 1984

Flint, Janet. *The Prints of Louis Lozowick: A Catalogue Raisonné*. New York, 1982

Foster, Milton P. 'The Reception of Max Nordau's 'Degeneration' in England and America'. PhD dissertation, University of Michigan, 1954

Frank, Herman. *Anarkho-sotsialistishe ideyen un bavegungen bay yidn: historishe un teorishe aynfirung* [Anarcho-Syndicalist Ideas and Movements Among Jews: A Historical and Theoretical Introduction]. Paris, 1951

Frankel, Jonathan. *The Damascus Affair: 'Ritual Murder', Politics, and the Jews in 1840*. Cambridge, 1997

——. 'Modern Jewish Politics East and West (1840–1939): Utopia, Myth, Reality'. In *Quest for Utopia*, ed. Gitelman, pp. 81–103

——. 'The Paradoxical Politics of Marginality: Thoughts on the Jewish Situation During the Years 1914–21'. *Studies in Contemporary Jewry*, IV (1988), pp. 3–21

——. *Prophecy and Politics: Socialism, Nationalism, and the Russian Jews, 1862–1917*. Cambridge, 1981

——, and Steven Zipperstein, eds. *Assimilation and Community: The Jews in Nineteenth-Century Europe*. Cambridge, 1992

Freedberg, David. *The Power of Images: Studies in the History and Theory of Response*. Chicago and London, 1991

Freedman, Russell. *Kids at Work: Lewis Hine and the Crusade Against Child Labor*. New York, 1994

Freidenreich, Harriet P. *Jewish Politics in Vienna 1918–1938*. Bloomington, 1991

Freund, Richard A. *Understanding Jewish Ethics*. San Francisco, 1990

Friedman, Alan J. and Carol C. Donley. *Einstein as Myth and Muse*. Cambridge, 1989

Friedman, Maurice. *Encounter on a Narrow Ridge: A Life of Martin Buber*. New York, 1991

——. *Martin Buber's Life and Work: The Early Years 1878–1923*. New York, 1981

Fussell, Paul. *The Great War and Modern Memory*. New York and London, 1975

Gabler, Neal. *An Empire of Their Own: How the Jews Invented Hollywood*. New York, 1989

Gal, Allon. 'Brandeis, Judaism, and Zionism'. In *Brandeis and America*, ed. Nelson L. Dawson. Lexington, KY, 1989, pp. 65-98

——. *Brandeis of Boston*. Cambridge, MA, 1980

——. 'Brandeis's View on the Upbuilding of Palestine, 1914–1923'. *Studies in Zionism*, 6 (Autumn 1982), pp. 216–38

——. 'Independence and Universal Mission in Modern Jewish Nationalism: Comparative Analysis of European and American Zionism (1897–1948)'. *Studies in Contemporary Jewry*, V (1989), pp. 242–74

——. 'Medinat yisrael haideialt be'einei 'hadassah', 1945–1955' [The Ideal State of Israel in the Eyes of Hadassah, 1945–1955]. *Yahadut Zémanenu*, 4 (1987), pp. 157–70

——. 'The Mission Motif in American Zionism (1898–1948)'. *American Jewish History*, 75 (June 1986), pp. 363–85

Gartner, Lloyd. *The Jewish Immigrant in England, 1870–1914*. London, 1960

Gaskell, Ivan. 'History of Images'. In *New Perspectives on Historical Writing*, ed. Peter Burke, pp. 168–92. University Park, PA, 1991

Gassman-Sherr, Rosalie. *The Story of the Federation of Women Zionists of Great Britain and Ireland*. London, 1968

Geller, Stuart. 'Louis D. Brandeis and Zionism'. Rabbinic thesis, Hebrew Union
College – Jewish Institute of Religion, Cincinnati, 1970

——. 'Why Did Louis D. Brandeis Choose Zionism?' *American Jewish Historical
Quarterly* (June 1973), pp. 383–499

Gellner, Ernest. *Nations and Nationalism*. Ithaca, 1992

Gidal, Nahum. 'Jews in Photography'. *Year Book of the Leo Baeck Institute*, XXXII
(1987), pp. 437–53

Giebels, Ludy, ed. *Jacob Israel De Haan: Correspondent in Palestina, 1919–1924*.
Special issue of *De Engelbewaarder*, 23 (July 1981)

——. 'Jacob Israel De Haan in Palestina, I'. *Studia Rosenthaliana*, XIV/1 (January
1980), pp. 44–78

——. 'Jacob Israel De Haan in Palestina,II'. *Studia Rosenthaliana*, XV/1 (March
1981), pp. 111–42

——. 'Jacob Israel De Haan in Palestina, III'. *Studia Rosenthaliana*, XV/2 (August
1981), pp. 188–233

Gilman, Sander. *Franz Kafka: The Jewish Patient*. New York, 1995

——. *Jewish Self-Hatred: Anti-Semitism and the Hidden Language of the Jews*.
Baltimore, 1986

——. *The Jew's Body*. New York and London, 1991

Gilner, Elias. *War and Hope: A History of the Jewish Legion*. New York, 1969

Gitelman, Zvi, ed. *The Quest for Utopia: Jewish Political Ideas and Institutions Through
the Ages*. Armonk, NY, 1992

Glenn, Susan A. *Daughters of the Shtetl: Life and Labor in the Immigrant Generation*.
London and Ithaca, 1990

Goldberg, J. J. and Elliot Kings, eds. *Builders and Dreamers: Habonim Labor Zionist
Youth in North America*. New York, 1993

Gombrich, E. H. *Aby Warburg: An Intellectual Biography*. Oxford, 1986

Gorny, Yosef. *The British Labour Movement and Zionism 1917–1948*. London, 1983

——. *The State of Israel in Jewish Public Thought: The Quest for Collective Identity*.
New York, 1994

Graur, Mina. *An Anarchist 'Rabbi': The Life and Teachings of Rudolf Rocker*. New York
and Jerusalem, 1997

Greene, Julie. *Pure and Simple: The American Federation of Labor and Political
Activism, 1881–1917*. Cambridge, 1998

Guha, Ranajit and Gayatri Chakroavorty Spivak, eds. *Selected Subaltern Studies*. New
York and Oxford, 1988

Gutman, Judith Mara. *Lewis W. Hine, 1874–1940: Two Perspectives*. New York, 1974

Haberer, Erich E. *Jews and Revolution in Nineteenth-Century Russia*. Cambridge, 1995

Habermas, Jurgen. *The Structural Transformation of the Public Sphere*. Trans. Thomas
Burger and Fredrick Lawrence. Cambridge, MA, 1989

Haimson, Leopold and Charles Tilly, eds. *Strikes, Wars, and Revolutions in
International Perspective: Strike Waves in the Late Nineteenth and Early Twentieth
Centuries*. Cambridge, 1989

Halbwachs, Maurice. *On Collective Memory*. Ed. and trans. Lewis Coser. Chicago,
1992

Halperin, Samuel. *The Political World of American Zionism*. Detroit, 1961

Halpern, Ben. *A Clash of Heroes: Brandeis, Weizmann and American Zionism*. New
York, 1985

——. *The Idea of the Jewish State*, 2nd rev. edn. Cambridge, MA, 1969

Hansen, Miriam. *Babel and Babylon: Spectatorship in American Silent Film*.
Cambridge, MA, and London, 1991

Harshav, Benjamin. *Language in Time of Revolution*. Berkeley, 1993

Hertzberg, Arthur, ed. *The Zionist Idea: A Historical Analysis and Reader*. New York, 1986

Higham, John, ed. *Ethnic Leadership in America*. Baltimore, 1978

——. *Send These to Me: Immigrants in Urban America*, rev. edn. Baltimore, 1984

Hobsbawm, E. J. *Nations and Nationalism Since 1780: Programme, Myth, Reality*. Cambridge, 1992

——, and Terence Ranger, eds. *The Invention of Tradition*. Cambridge, 1983

Hodess, Jacob. 'Tsu der geshikhte fun der english-yiddish presse' [On the History of the Anglo-Yiddish Press]. In *Yidn in England: studies un materialn 1880–1940*, pp. 40⁻71. New York, 1940

Hoff, Mascha. *Johann Kremenezky und die Gruendung des KKLs*. Frankfurt a.M., 1986

Hofmann, Werner, Georg Syamken, and Martin Warnke. *Die Menschenrechte des Auges: Über Aby Warburg*. Frankfurt a.M., 1980

Hofstadter, Richard. *The American Political Tradition and the Men Who Made It*. New York, 1960

——. *Anti-Intellectualism in American Life*. New York, 1963

Holly, Michael Ann. *Panofsky and the Foundations of Art History*. Ithaca, 1984

Holton, Gerald and Yehuda Elkana, eds. *Albert Einstein: Historical and Cultural Perspectives*. Princeton, 1982

Holub, Robert. *Reception Theory: A Critical Introduction*. London and New York, 1984

Horowitz, Elliot. 'Visages du judaism: de la barbe en monde juif et de l'élaboration de ses significations'. *Annales Histoire, Sciences Sociales*, 49 (1994), pp. 1080–6

Howe, Irving. *World of Our Fathers: The Journey of the East European Jews to America and the Life They Found and Made*. New York and London, 1976

Howes, Justin and Pauline Paucker. 'German Jews and the Graphic Arts'. *Year Book of Leo Baeck Institute*, XXXIV (1989), pp. 443–74

Huntington-Whiteley, James, ed. *The Book of British Sporting Heroes*. London, 1998

Hyman, Paula E. *Gender and Assimilation in Modern Jewish History: The Roles and Representation of Women*. Seattle and London, 1995

——. 'Was There a "Jewish Politics" in Western and Central Europe?'. In *Quest for Utopia*, ed. Gitelman, pp. 105–17

Isenberg, Noah. *Between Redemption and Doom: The Strains of German–Jewish Modernism*. Lincoln, NE, 1999

Iser, Wolfgang. 'The Repertoire'. In *Critical Theory Since 1965*, ed. Hazard Adams and Leroy Searle, pp. 360–80. Tallahassee, FL, 1986

Jacobs, Rose. 'Beginnings of Hadassah'. In *Early History of Zionism in America*, ed. Isidor S. Meyer, pp. 228–44. New York, 1977

Jauss, Hans Robert. *Literatur als Provokation*. Frankfurt a.M., 1972

Joll, James. *The Anarchists*, 2nd edn. London, 1979

Kadish, Sharman. *Bolsheviks and British Jews: The Anglo–Jewish Community, Britain, and the Russian Revolution*. London, 1992

Kahan, Arcadius. *Essays in Jewish Social and Economic History*. Ed. Roger Weiss. London and Chicago, 1986

Kaplan, Marion. *Between Dignity and Despair: Jewish Life in Nazi Germany*. New York, 1998

——. *The Jewish Feminist Movement in Germany: The Campaigns of the Jüdischer Frauenbund, 1904–1938*. Westport, CT, 1979

——. *The Making of the Jewish Middle Class: Women, Family, and Identity in Imperial Germany*. New York and Oxford, 1991

Kaplan, Wendy, ed. *Designing Modernity: The Arts of Reform and Persuasion*

1885–1945. New York, 1995

Karp, Abraham, J. *To Give Life: The UJA in the Shaping of the American Jewish Community*. New York, 1981

Katz, Jacob. *From Prejudice to Destruction: Anti-Semitism 1700–1933*. Cambridge, MA, 1982

——. *Out of the Ghetto: The Social Background of Jewish Emancipation*. New York, 1978

Kepnes, Steven, ed. *Interpreting Judaism in a Postmodern Age*. New York, 1995

Kershen, Anne J. *United the Tailors: Trade Unionism Amongst the Tailoring Workers of London and Leeds, 1870–1939*. London, 1995

Kleeblatt, Norman L., ed. *The Dreyfus Affair, Art, Truth, and Justice*. Berkeley, 1987

——. *Too Jewish?: Challenging Traditional Identities*. New York and New Brunswick, NJ, 1996

Klein, Dennis B. *Jewish Origins of the Psychoanalytic Movement*. Chicago and London, 1985

Klier, John. *Imperial Russia's Jewish Question, 1855–1881*. Cambridge, 1995

Knee, Stuart. *The Concept of Zionist Dissent in the American Mind, 1917–1941*. New York, 1979

Koch, Stephen. *Stalin, Willi Muenzenberg and the Seduction of the Intellectuals*. London, 1995

Kohn, Hans. *Living in a World Revolution*. New York, 1964

Kornberg, Jacques, ed. *At the Crossroads: Essays on Ahad Ha-Am*. Albany, 1983

——. *Theodor Herzl: From Assimilation to Zionism*. Bloomington, 1993

Kress, Gunther and Theo van Leeuwen, *Reading Images: The Grammar of Visual Design*. London and New York, 1996

Kugelmass, Jack. 'Jewish Icons: Envisioning the Self in Images of the Other'. In *Jews and Other Differences*, ed. Boyarin and Boyarin, pp. 30–53

——. *The Miracle of Intervale Avenue: The Story of a Jewish Congregation in the South Bronx*. New York, 1996

Kutscher, Carol Bosworth. 'The Early Years of Hadassah 1912–1921'. PhD dissertation, Brandeis University, 1976

Kuzmack, Linda Gordon. *Women's Cause: The Jewish Women's Movement in England and the United States 1881–1939*. Columbus, 1990

Lamberti, Marjorie. 'From Coexistence to Conflict: Zionism and the Jewish Community in Germany, 1899–1914'. *Year Book of the Leo Baeck Institute*, XXVII (1982), pp. 53–86

Langemann, Ellen Condliffe. *A Generation of Women: Education in the Lives of Progressive Reformers*. Cambridge, MA, and London, 1979

Lavsky, Hagit. *Before Catastrophe: The Distinctive Path of German Zionism*. Detroit and Jerusalem, 1996

Lederhendler, Eli. *Jewish Responses to Modernity: New Voices in America and Eastern Europe*. New York and London, 1994

——. *The Road to Modern Jewish Politics: Political Tradition and Political Reconstruction in the Jewish Community of Tsarist Russia*. Oxford, 1989

Leppert, Richard. *Art and the Committed Eye: The Cultural Functions of Imagery*. Boulder, 1995

Levene, Mark. *War, Jews, and the New Europe: The Diplomacy of Lucien Wolf 1914–1919*. Oxford, 1992

Levine, Lawrence W. 'The Historian and the Icon: Photography and the History of American People in the 1930s and 1940s'. In *Modern Art and Society: An Anthology of Social and Multicultural Readings*, ed. Maurice Berger, pp. 173–200. New York, 1994

Lewis, Marx. *Meyer London*. New York, 1975

Lewis, Morton. *Ted Kid Lewis: His Life and Times*. London, 1990

Lidtke, Vernon L. *The Alternative Culture: Socialist Labor in Imperial Germany*. New York, 1985

Loewy, Michael. *Redemption and Utopia. Jewish Libertarian Thought in Central Europe: A Study in Elective Affinity*. Trans. Hope Heaney. Stanford, 1992

Louis Lozowick: American Precisionist Retrospective, February 26–May 7, 1978. Long Beach, 1978

Lowenthal, David. *The Past Is a Foreign Country*. Cambridge, 1985

Lowenthal, Marvin, ed., *The Diaries of Theodor Herzl*. Gloucester, MA, 1978.

McCartin, Joseph A. *Labor's Great War: The Struggle for Industrial Democracy and the Origins of Modern American Labor Relations, 1912–1921*. Chapel Hill, 1987

Maimon, Ada. *Women Built a Land*. Trans. Shulamith Schwarz-Nardi. New York, 1962

Manor-Friedman, Tamar, ed. *Workers and Revolutionaries: The Jewish Labor Movement*. Tel Aviv, 1994

Marmorstein, Emile. *Heaven at Bay: The Jewish Kulturkampf in the Holy Land*. London and New York, 1969

——. *A Martyr's Message: To Commemorate the Fiftieth Anniversary of the Murder of Professor De-Haan*. London, 1975

Marrus, Michael. *The Politics of Assimilation: A Study of the French Jewish Community at the Time of the Dreyfus Affair*. Oxford, 1971

Martin, Sean. 'Ambivalent Opposition: Jewish Political Power in Poland, 1926–1928'. MA thesis, Ohio State University, 1994

Mattenklott, Gert. *Bilderdienst*. Munich, 1976

Maurer, Trude. *Die Entwicklung der jüdische Minderheit in Deutschland 1780–1933: neuere Forschungen und offene Fragen*. Tübingen, 1992

——. *Ostjuden in Deutschland 1918–1933*. Hamburg, 1986

Medding, Peter Y. 'The 'New Jewish Politics' in the United States: Historical Perspectives'. In *Quest for Utopia*, ed. Gitelman, pp. 119–53

——. 'The Politics of Jewry as a Mobilized Diaspora'. In *Culture, Ethnicity, and Identity: Current Issues in Research*, ed. William C. Mcready, pp. 195–207. New York, 1983

Meijer, Jaap. *De Zoon van een Gazzen: het leven van Jacob Israel de Haan, 1881–1924*. Amsterdam, 1967

Mendelsohn, Ezra. *Class Struggle in the Pale: The Formative Years of the Jewish Workers' Movement in Tsarist Russia*. Cambridge, 1970

——, ed. *Essential Papers on Jews and Left*. New York and London, 1997

——. *The Jews of East Central Europe Between the Wars*. Bloomington, 1987

——. *On Modern Jewish Politics*. New York, 1993

——. *Zionism in Poland: The Formative Years, 1915–1926*. New Haven, 1981

Meshi-Zahav, Tsevi and Yehudah Meshi-Zahav. *ha-Kadosh. Rabi Ya'akov Yisrael Deh-Han ha-y.d.: ha-retsah ha-Tsiyoni harishon be-e. Y.* [The Martyr, Rabbi Jacob Israel De Haan: The First Zionist Murder in Eretz Israel]. Jerusalem, 1986

Meyer, Michael with Michael Brenner, eds. *German–Jewish History in Modern Times, vol. 3: Integration in Dispute*. New York, 1997

——. *German–Jewish History in Modern Times, vol. 4: Renewal and Destruction: 1918–1945*. New York, 1998

Miller, Donald H. 'A History of Hadassah 1912–1935'. PhD dissertation, New York University, 1968

Mink, Gwendolyn. *Old Labor and New Immigrants in American Political Development: Union, Party, and State, 1875–1920*. Ithaca, 1986

Mitchell, W.J.T. *Iconology: Image, Text, Ideology.* Chicago and London, 1987
——. *Picture Theory: Essays on Verbal and Visual Representation.* Chicago, 1984
Mittleman, Alan. *The Politics of Torah: The Jewish Political Tradition and the Founding of Agudat Israel.* Albany, 1996
Montgomery, David. *Citizen Workers: The Experience of Workers in the United States with Democracy and the Free Market During the Nineteenth Century.* Cambridge, 1993
——. *The Fall of the House of Labor: The Workplace, the State and American Labor Activism, 1865–1925.* Cambridge, 1987
Morton, James. *Gangland: London's Underworld.* London, 1998
Mosse, George. *Confronting the Nation: Jewish and Western Nationalism.* Hanover, NH, 1993
——. *The Crisis of German Ideology.* New York, 1981
——. *German Jews Beyond Judaism.* Bloomington, 1988
——. 'The Influence of the Volkish Idea on German Jewry'. In *Germans and Jews: The Right, the Left, and the Search for a 'Third Force' in Pre-War Germany*, pp. 77–115. Detroit, 1987
——. *The Jews and the German War Experience 1914–1918.* New York, 1977
——. *Nationalism and Sexuality: Respectability and Abnormal Sexuality in Modern Europe.* New York, 1985
——, ed. *Nazi Culture: Intellectual, Cultural, and Social Life in the Third Reich.* New York, 1966
Myers, David. *Re-inventing the Jewish Past: European Jewish Intellectuals and the Zionist Return to History.* New York, 1995
Nakdimon, Shlomoh. *Deh Han: ha-retsah ha-politi ha-rishon be-Erets-Yisrael* [De Haan: The First Political Assassination in Eretz Israel]. Tel Aviv, 1985
Navon, Yitzhak. 'On Einstein and the Presidency of Israel'. In *Albert Einstein*, ed. Holton and Elkana. Princeton, 1982
Negt, Oskar and Alexander Kluge, *Public Sphere and Experience: Toward an Analysis of the Bourgeois and Proletarian Public Sphere.* Foreword by Miriam Hansen, trans. Peter Labanyi, Jamie Owen Daniel, and Assenka Oksiloff. Minneapolis and London, 1993
Nicosia, Francis. *The Third Reich and the Palestine Question.* Austin, 1985
Nochlin, Linda, and Tamar Garb, eds. *The Jew in the Text: Modernity and the Construction of Identity.* London, 1995
Novick, Peter. *That Noble Dream: The 'Objectivity Question' and the American Historical Profession.* Cambridge, 1993
Oliver, Hermia. *The International Anarchist Movement in Late Victorian London.* London, 1983
Orleck, Annelise. *Common Sense and a Little Fire: Women and Working-Class Politics in the United States, 1900–1965.* Chapel Hill and London, 1995
Pais, Abraham. *Subtle Is the Lord: The Science and Life of Albert Einstein.* New York, 1982
Paret, Peter. *Art as History: Episodes in the Culture and Politics of Nineteenth-Century Germany.* Princeton, 1988
Parzen, Herbert. 'The United Palestine Appeal'. *Herzl Year Book*, VII (1971), pp. 355–93
Pawel, Ernst. *The Labyrinth of Exile: A Life of Theodor Herzl.* New York, 1989
——. *The Nightmare of Reason: A Life of Franz Kafka.* New York, 1984
Penslar, Derek. *Zionism and Technocracy: The Engineering of Jewish Settlement in Palestine.* Indianapolis and Bloomington, 1991
Pickus, Keith. *Constructing Modern Identities: Jewish University Students in Germany*

1815–1914. Detroit, 1999

Pohl, Frances K. *In the Eye of the Storm. An Art of Conscience 1930–1970: Selections from the Collection of Philip J. & Suzanne Schiller*. San Francisco, 1995

Poppel, Stephen M. *Zionism in Germany 1897–1933: The Shaping of a Jewish Identity*. Philadelphia, 1977

Postal, Bernard, Jesse Silver, and Roy Silver. *Encyclopedia of Jews in Sports*. New York, 1965

Prestel, Claudia. 'Frauen und die Zionistische Bewegung (1897–1933): Tradition oder Revolution?'. *Historische Zeitschrift*, 258 (1994), pp. 29–71

Pulzer, Peter. *The Rise of Political Anti-Semitism in Germany and Austria*, rev. edn. Cambridge. MA, 1988

Rabin, Else. 'The Jewish Women in Social Service in Germany'. In *The Jewish Library, vol. III*, ed. Leo Jung, pp. 268–310. New York, 1934

Rabinbach, Anson and Jack Zipes, eds. *Germans and Jews Since the Holocaust*. New York, 1986

Rabinowicz, Oscar K. *Fifty Years of Zionism: A Historical Analysis of Dr Weizmann's 'Trial and Error'*. London, 1950

Raphael, Marc Lee. *A History of the United Jewish Appeal, 1939–1982*. Providence, 1982

Rapoport-Albert, Ada, ed. *Hasidism Reappraised*. London and Portland, OR, 1997

——, and Steven Zipperstein, eds. *Jewish History: Essays in Honour of Chimen Abramsky*. London, 1988

Reinharz, Jehuda. *Chaim Weizmann: The Making of a Statesman*. New York, 1993

——. *Chaim Weizmann: The Making of a Zionist Leader*. New York, 1985

——, ed. *Dokumente zur Geschichte des deutschen Zionismus 1882–1933*. Tübingen, 1981

——. *Fatherland or Promised Land: The Dilemma of the German Jew, 1893–1914*. Ann Arbor, 1975

——. 'Science in the Service of Politics: The Case of Chaim Weizmann During the First World War'. *English Historical Review* (July 1985), pp. 572–603

——, and Paul Mendes-Flohr, eds. *The Jew in the Modern World: A Documentary History*, 2nd edn. New York, 1995

Richarz, Monika, ed. *Bürger auf Widerruf: Lebenszeugnisse deutscher Juden 1780–1945*. Munich, 1989

——, ed. *Jewish Life in Germany: Memoirs from Three Centuries*. Trans. Stella P. Rosenfeld and Sidney Rosenfeld. Bloomington and Indianapolis, 1991

Rischin, Moses. *The Promised City: New York's Jews, 1870–1914*. Cambridge, MA, and London, 1977

Robertson, Ritchie. *Heine*. New York, 1988

Rocker, Rudolf. *Johann Most: das Leben eines Rebellen*. Berlin, 1924

Rodrigue, Aron. *Images of Sephardi and Eastern Jewries in Transition: The Teachers of the Alliance Israélite Universelle*. London and Seattle, 1993

Rollin, Aaron R. 'Bletlekh tsu der geshikhte fun der yidisher arbeter-bavegung in England'. In *Yidn in England: studies un materialn 1880–1940* [Notes on the history of the Jewish labour movement in England], pp. 273–82. New York, 1940

Rose, Norman. *Chaim Weizmann: A Biography*. New York, 1986

Roskies, David G. *Against the Apocalypse: Responses to Catastrophe in Modern Jewish Culture*. Cambridge, MA, and London, 1984

Roth, Philip. *American Pastoral*. London, 1998

Rozenblit, Marsha L. 'The Assertion of Identity: Jewish Student Nationalism at the University of Vienna Before the First World War'. *Year Book of the Leo Baeck Institute*, XXVII (1982), pp. 171–86

——. *The Jews of Vienna: Assimilation and Identity, 1870–1914*. Albany, 1983

Rudolf Rocker: A Memorial. Special issue of *The Dandelion*, IV/14 (Summer 1980)

Sachar, Howard M. *A History of the Jews in America*. New York, 1992

Said, Edward. *Culture and Imperialism*. New York, 1993

——. *Orientalism*. New York, 1976

——. *The Question of Palestine*. New York, 1980

Sanders, Ronald. *The Downtown Jews: Portraits of an Immigrant Generation*. New York, 1987

Sarna, Jonathon. *JPS. The Americanization of Jewish Culture: 1888–1988*. Philadelphia, 1989

Schmidt, Peter. *Aby M. Warburg und die Ikonologie*. Bamberg, 1989

Schorske, Carl E. *Fin-de-Siècle Vienna: Politics and Culture*. New York, 1981

Schulte, Christoph. *Psychopathologie des fin-de-siècle: der Kulturkritiker, Arzt und Zionist Max Nordau*. Frankfurt a. M., 1997

Scott, Joan Wallach. *Gender and the Politics of History*. New York, 1988

——. 'Women's History'. In *New Perspectives on Historical Writing*, ed. Peter Burke, pp. 42–66. State College, PA, 1991

Segev, Tom. *The Seventh Million: The Israelis and the Holocaust*. Trans. Haim Watzman. New York, 1992

Sekula, Alan. *Photography Against the Grain: Essays and Photo Works, 1973–1983*. Halifax, 1984

Shapira, Anita. *Berl: The Biography of a Socialist Zionist*. Trans. Haya Galai. New York, 1984

——. *Land and Power: The Zionist Resort to Force, 1881–1948*. Trans. William Templer. New York, 1992

Shapiro, Leon. *The History of ORT: A Jewish Movement for Social Change*. New York, 1980

Shapiro, Robert D. *A Reform Rabbi in the Progressive Era: The Early Career of Stephen S. Wise*. New York and London, 1988

Shapiro, Yonathan. *Leadership of the American Zionist Organization 1897–1930*. Urbana, 1971

Sharfman, Glenn R. 'The Jewish Youth Movement in Germany, 1900–1936: A Study in Ideology and Organization'. PhD dissertation, University of North Carolina, 1989

Shavit, Yaacov. *Jabotinsky and the Revisionist Movement 1925–1948*. London, 1988

Shilo, Margalit. 'The Women's Farm at Kinneret, 1911–1917: A Solution to the Problem of Working Women in the Second Aliya'. *Jerusalem Cathedre* (1981), pp. 246–83

Shilo-Cohen, Nurit, ed. *Bezalel 1906–1929*. Jerusalem, 1983

Shimoni, Gideon. *Jews and Zionism: The South African Experience, 1910–1967*. New York, 1980

——. 'Poale Zion: A Zionist Transplant in Britain (1905–1945)'. *Studies in Contemporary Jewry*, II (1986), pp. 227–69

——. *The Zionist Ideology*. Hanover, NH, 1995

Silberstein, Laurence. 'Cultural Criticism, Ideology, and the Interpretation of Zionism: Toward a Post-Zionist Discourse'. In *Interpreting Judaism in a Postmodern Age*, ed. Steven Kepnes, pp. 325–58. New York, 1996

Simon, Leon. *Ahad Ha-Am*. Philadelphia, 1960

Slowe, Peter. *Manny Shinwell: An Authorised Biography*. London and Boulder, 1993

Smith, Anthony D. *The Ethnic Origins of Nations*. Oxford and Cambridge, MA, 1993

Sokolow, Florian. *Nahum Sokolow: Life and Legend*. London, 1975

Sokolow, Nahum. *History of Zionism 1600–1918*. New York, 1969

Sontag, Susan. *On Photography*. Harmondsworth, 1979

Sorin, Gerald. *The Jewish People in America, vol. III: A Time For Building: The Third Migration 1880–1920*. Baltimore and London, 1992

——. *The Prophetic Minority: American Jewish Immigrant Radicals, 1880–1920*. Bloomington, 1984

Sorkin, David. *The Transformation of the German Jewry, 1780–1840*. New York, 1990

Soyer, Daniel. *Jewish Immigrant Associations and American Identity in New York, 1880–1939*. London and Cambridge, MA, 1997

Stanislawski, Michael. *For Whom Do I Toil?: Judah Lieb Gordon and the Crisis of Russian Jewry*. New York, 1988

Stapert-Eggen, Marijke T. C. 'The Rosenthaliana's Jacob Israel de Haan Archive'. In *Bibliotheca Rosenthaliana. Treasures of Jewish Booklore: Marking the 200th Anniversary of the Birth of Leeser Rosenthal, 1794–1994*, ed. Emile G. L. Schrijver and F. J. Hoogewoud, pp. 98–9. Amsterdam, 1994

Steinberg, Michael P. 'Aby Warburg's Kruezlingen Lecture: A Reading'. In Aby Warburg, *Images from the Region of the Pueblo Indians of North America*, trans. and ed. Michael P. Steinberg, pp. 59–114. Ithaca and London, 1995

——, ed. *Walter Benjamin and the Demands of History*. Ithaca and London, 1996

Steinweis, Alan E. *Art, Ideology, and Economics in Nazi Germany: The Reich Chambers of Music, Theater, and the Visual Arts*. Chapel Hill, 1993

Stock, Ernest. *Partners and Pursestrings: A History of the United Israel Appeal*. Lanham, MD, 1987

Strange, Maren. *Symbols of Ideal Life: Social Documentary Photography in America 1890–1950*. Cambridge, 1992

Strum, Philippa. *Brandeis: Beyond Progressivism*. Lawrence, KS, 1993

——. *Louis D. Brandeis: Justice of the People*. Cambridge, MA, 1984

Sussman, Warren. *Culture as History: The Transformation of American Society in the Twentieth Century*. New York, 1984

Tagg, John. *The Burden of Representation: Essays on Photographies and Histories*. Amherst, MA, 1988

Tananbaum, Susan. 'Generations of Change: The Anglicization of Russian-Jewish Immigrant Women in London, 1880–1939'. PhD dissertation, Brandeis University, 1991

Tartakover, David, ed. *Herzl in Profile: Herzl's Image in the Applied Arts*. Tel Aviv, 1979

Thomas, Richard D. 'Joseph Barondess: Labor Leader and Humanitarian'. MA thesis, Ohio State University, 1958

Tomlins, Christopher L. *The State and the Unions: Labor Relations, Law, and the Organized Labor Movement in America, 1880–1960*. Cambridge, 1985

Tscherikower, E., ed. *Geshikhte fun der yidisher arbeter-bavegung in de fareynikte shtatn* [History of the Jewish workers' movement in the United States], II. New York, 1945

Urofsky, Melvin. *American Zionism from Herzl to the Holocaust*. Garden City, NY, 1975

——. *A Voice That Spoke for Justice: The Life and Times of Stephen S. Wise*. Albany, 1982

——. *We Are One!: American Jewry and Israel*. Garden City, NY, 1978

Vital, David. *The Future of the Jews*. Cambridge, MA, 1990

——. *The Origins of Zionism*. Oxford, 1975

——. *Zionism: The Crucial Phase*. Oxford, 1987

——. *Zionism: The Formative Years*. Oxford, 1982

Weinberg, David H. *Between Tradition and Modernity: Haim Zhitlowski, Simon Dubnow, Ahad Ha-Am, and the Shaping of Modern Jewish Identity*. New York and

London, 1996

Wertheimer, Jack, ed. *The Modern Jewish Experience: A Reader's Guide*. New York and London, 1993

——. *Unwelcome Strangers: East European Jews in Imperial Germany*. New York and Oxford, 1987

White, Hayden. *The Content of the Form: Narrative Discourse and Historical Representation*. London and Baltimore, 1992

Wigoder, Geoffrey, ed. *Dictionary of Jewish Biography*. New York, 1991

Williams, Bill. *The Making of Manchester Jewry, 1740–1875*. New York, 1976

Wilson, Nelly. *Bernard Lazare: Antisemitism and the Problem of Jewish Identity in Late Nineteenth-Century France*. Cambridge, 1978

Wistrich, Robert S. *The Jews of Vienna in the Age of Franz Joseph*. Oxford, 1990

——. 'Theodor Herzl: The Making of a Political Messiah'. In *The Shaping of Israeli Identity: Myth, Memory, and Trauma*, ed. Robert Wistrich and David Ohana, pp. 1–37. London and Portland, OR, 1995

——. *A Weekend in Munich: Art, Propaganda, and Terror in the Third Reich*. London, 1995

Wyman, David S. *The Abandonment of the Jews: America and the Holocaust, 1941–1945*. New York, 1985

Yerushalmi, Yosef. *Zakhor: Jewish History and Jewish Memory*. New York, 1982

Yisraeli, David. 'The Struggle for Zionist Military Involvement in the First World War, 1914–1917'. In *Bar Ilan Studies in History*, ed. Pinhas Artzi. 1978

Young, James E. *The Texture of Memory: Holocaust Memorials and Meaning*. New Haven, 1993

Yudkin, Leon. *Jewish Writing and Identity in the Twentieth Century*. London, 1982

Zeitlin, Rose. *Henrietta Szold*. New York, 1952

Zerubavel, Yael. *Recovered Roots: Collective Memory and the Making of Israeli National Tradition*. Chicago, 1995

Zipperstein, Steven. *Elusive Prophet: Ahad Ha-Am and the Origins of Zionism*. Berkeley, 1993

——. 'The Politics of Relief: The Transformation of Russian Jewish Communal Life During the First World War'. *Studies in Contemporary Jewry*, IV (1988), pp. 22–40

Photographic Acknowledgements

The author and publishers wish to express their thanks to the following sources of illustrative material and/or permission to reproduce it and/or permission to take photographs and reproduce them:

American Jewish Archives, Cincinnati, OH: 1, 15, 16, 25, 32, 50, 78–80, 84, 89, 99, 100; Edmonton/American Jewish Archives: 100; Halsman/American Jewish Archives: 31; Pershie/American Jewish Archives: 79; British Library, London: 17, 87, 88; Central Zionist Archives, Jerusalem: frontispiece, 5, 6, 9, 10, 11, 12, 13, 14, 19, 27, 30, 33–7, 39–49, 51–64, 67–72, 75–7, 81–3; Emil Buri/Central Zionist Archives: 38; Forward Association, New York: 2, 101–3; Joods Historisch Museum, Amsterdam: 74; Jewish Museum, Finchley, London: 26, 73, 86, 104–5; Jewish National and University Library, Hebrew University of Jerusalem: 8; Ohio State University Library and Ohio State Media Services, Columbus, OH: 4, 21, 23–4, 66, 90–98; Private collection, London/Ohio State University Library and Ohio State Media Services: 28–9, 85; Workmen's Circle, New York: 3, 18, 22, 65; Wiener Library, Tel Aviv: 7, 20.

Index